FOREWORD

by
Francesco Frangialli,
Secretary-General

The World Tourism Organization has developed a unique system of information in the field of tourism. This publication on tourism signs and symbols and visitor signage is one of its results.

Today, globalization leads to ever-more frequent encounters between peoples educated under different cultural systems, with speech and customs that are so diverse that no universal language could easily reconcile them. Universal human communication, however, has existed since the dawn of creation. It began with signs and signals, gestures that civilizations as ancient as the Chinese or Egyptian reflected in ideograms or hieroglyphs.

In a multifarious world whose transformation is becoming more widespread under the effects of the expansion of the information society and new communication technologies, common languages in images must be devised to facilitate the movement of persons and improve the safety, security and comfort of the users of tourism facilities and sites. Images, words, objects and ideas represented by symbols can be widely understood if they are simple and meet universal needs. This development engenders keener demand not only for information and the quality of hospitality offered, but also for the promotion and identity of territories, areas and heritage sites with a tourism vocation, as well as the advertising and identification of tourism enterprises whose tendency to become transnational is gathering pace.

This need for universal communication, irrespective of language, is enshrined as a fundamental principle in the Manila Declaration on World Tourism adopted on 17 September 1980. The use of symbols for depicting tourist attractions is a decisive step in this direction. The WTO Secretariat has gathered an exhaustive set of signs and symbols that have either been or could be standardized internationally, as well

i

as trademarks and colours relevant to the safety, security and comfort of tourists and users of tourism and transport facilities and infrastructure.

The Guide we are presenting to you here is an essential source of information, addressing as it does the issue of signs and symbols linked to travel and to tourism signage. It is the outcome of a survey carried out among national tourism administrations worldwide and such international organizations as IMO, ICAO, FIA and ISO, which deal directly or indirectly with this subject. It is a source of knowledge and support for planners, developers, marketing experts and all those responsible for communications in tourism or tourism-related organizations and enterprises. This Guide sets out the concepts and terminology used in this field, as well as more than 290 potential symbols for public and tourist information, which are in the process of being harmonized as part of WTO's cooperation with other international organizations.

Madrid, April 2001

109991

BCFTCS

$30.00

TOURISM SIGNS & SYMBOLS

ATIVE STUDIES

A Status Report & Handbook

Copyright © 2001 World Tourism Organization

TOURISM SIGNS AND SYMBOLS
A Status Report & Guidebook

ISBN: 92-844-0378-2

Published by the World Tourism Organization

All rights reserved. No part of this book may be reproduced or
transmitted in any form or by any means, electronic or mechani-
cal, including photocopying, recording or by any information storage and retrieval system without permission from the World
Tourism Organization.

The designations employed and the presentation of material in
this publication do not imply the expression of any opinions what-
soever on the part of the Secretariat of the World Tourism
Organization concerning the legal status of any country, territory,
city or area or of its authorities or concerning the delimitation of
its frontiers or boundaries.

ACKNOWLEDGMENTS

For the preparation of this publication, the WTO Secretariat requested information from other international sources such as the International Organization for Standardization (ISO), the International Automobile Federation (IFA), the World Intellectual Property Organization (WIPO), the Asia Pacific Economic Cooperation (APEC), the International Maritime Organization (IMO), the International Civil Aviation Organization (ICAO) and the International Railroads Union.

The WTO Secretariat would like to extend its sincere thanks to the member States and international governmental and non-governmental organizations that have helped in the preparation of this publication, especially the International Federation of Tour Operators (IFTO) which informed WTO in early 1997 of the danger arising out of confusion caused by the different colours of beach warning flags on the world's beaches.

This Status Report and Guidebook was drawn up with the collaboration of a consultant, Prof. Robert Lanquar, Ph.D. The draft was reviewed and consolidated by Henryk Handszuh and formatted by Eril Wiehahn and Carmen López-Lahesa (WTO Secretariat).

B.C.F.T.C.S.
109991

CONTENTS

CHAPTER II
INTERNATIONAL COOPERATION IN THE FIELD OF PUBLIC
AND TOURISM SIGNAGE 53

CHAPTER III
SELECTED SIGNS AND SYMBOLS STANDARDIZED, RECOMMENDED
AND USED FOR PUBLIC AND VISITOR INFORMATION 75

ACRONYMS AND ABBREVIATIONS

AARP	American Association of Retired Persons
AENOR	Spanish Association for Standardization
	(Asociación Española de Normalización)
AFIT	French Agency for Tourism Engineering
	(Agence française pour l'Ingénierie touristique)
AFNOR	French Agency for Standardization
	(Agence française de normalisation)
AH&MA	American Hotel and Motel Association
ALPE	Spanish Association against Poliomyelitis
ANSI	American National Standards Institute
APEC	Asia Pacific Economic Cooperation
APEC/TWG	APEC Tourism Working Group
BSI	British Standards Institution
COPANT	Pan-American Commission for Technical Standards
CSBTS	China State Bureau of Quality and Technical Supervision
DGNT	General Direction for Standardization (Mexico)
FIA	International Automobile Federation
	(Fédération internationale de l'Automobile)
ICAO	International Civil Aviation Organization
IFTO	International Federation of Tour Operators
IMO	International Maritime Organization
INDECOP	National Institute for Competition and Intellectual Property
	Protection (Peru)
INN	National Institute for Standardization (Chile)
IOC	International Olympic Committee
ISO	International Organization for Standardization
ISO/TC	ISO Technical Committee
JISC	Japanese Industrial Standards Committee c/o Standards
	Department, MITI
KNITQ	Korean National Institute of Technology and Quality
NTA	National Tourism Administration
NTO	National Tourism Office or Organization
RI	Rehabilitation International
RIS	Network of Info Bays - Réseau d'Info Stations
SAA	Standards Australia
SADC	South Africa Development Community

SCC	Standard Council of Canada
SNZ	Standards New Zealand
TISI	Thai Industrial Standards Institute
TRIPS	Trade Related Intellectual Property Rights
UIC	International Railroads Union
	(Union internationale des chemins de fer)
UNCRT	United Nations Conference on Road Traffic
UNDP	United Nations Development Programme
UNIT	Uruguayan Institute for Technical Norms
	(Instituto Uruguayo de normas técnicas)
WIPO	World Intellectual Property Organization
WTO	World Tourism Organization
WTO/OMC	World Trade Organization

MAIN TERMS USED

Sign: The term " sign " denotes a mark, device or symbol used to be perceived and which allows to represent or to distinguish things, objects, concepts or places.

Signal: A sound , light or body sign.

Symbol: A visually perceptible figure, reproduced by means of writing, drawing, painting or other manufacturing technique, intended to convey a particular meaning.

Graphical or graphic symbol: a visually perceptible figure used to transmit information independently of language. It may be produced by drawing, printing or other means.

Public information symbol: graphical symbol, intended to give information to the general public, the understanding of which is not normally dependent on specialist or occupational training.

Marker: graphic sign used to indicate position on ground to aircraft, course at sea to boats, on poles or trees for ski slopes and trails, paths, etc.

Icon: A sign creating an analogy and resemblance with the object in question and allowing a link to facilitate computer tasks (macro-link in a computer program).

Indication: A sign that relates to the material object (smoke indicates fire, movement of the weathervane indicates wind, etc.).

Referent: The subject represented by the symbol and a concise verbal message of the meaning of the proposed symbol.

A **Variant** is an alternative symbol design for a given referent.

Tourist attractions: the places and events which may be of interest to individuals in the utilization of their free time, whether active or passive, and which are outside their everyday environment and usual needs both of trade, accommodation, food and services.
Tourist facilities: the establishments, buildings, equipment used by visitors during their travel.

Logo or logotype: an emblem or device chosen as a badge of organization or company in display material: advertisement, promotion, head letter paper, etc.

Trade mark: device or word(s) that are legally registered or already established to name the goods and services of an organization, factory or company. "Any sign capable of distinguishing the goods and services of one undertaking from those of other undertakings shall be capable of constituting a trade mark". (Agreement on Trade Related Aspects of Intellectual Property Rights (TRIPS) of the World Trade Organization and the World Intellectual Property Organization, Geneva, 1994).

Copyright: symbol securing the legal right to reproduce, publish or sell a work or part of a work in literature, music or art such as a logo, sign, icon.

One notices the use of the terms " sign ", " symbol ", " graphical symbol ", " device ", " figure ", of which " symbol " appears to be the common denominator. Conventionally, the term " symbol " will be mainly used. But other definitions and terms may appear in documents proposed by countries such as pictogram or ideogram. The former (pictogram) is a drawing suggesting an activity, service or facility without any mention of a trademark or signature; the latter (ideogram) is a sign that is placed before an indication to a destination in order to characterize the type of destination.

INTRODUCTION

This publication capitalizes on the 1998-2000 activities of the World Tourism Organization corresponding to its Quality of Tourism Development programme, in particular under a section on technical standards.

The Quality Support Committee of WTO dealt with tourism signs and symbols at its fourth meeting (Madrid, Spain, 12-13 April 2000). It proposed a series of recommendations of the Council (included in this report as annex 7) which the latter accepted on 30 November 2000 by decision CE(DEC/6(LXIII-LXIX).

The decision to publish the results of the work done so far has been prompted by a few factors: an increasing number of inquiries about tourism signs and symbols and technical cooperation requests from member and non-member States of WTO as well as tourism industry organizations, renewed interest in public information symbols by the International Organization for Standardization (ISO) and, last but not least, the requirements of globalization fuelled by both information technologies and tourism. Both need effective communication tools such as culturally-friendly and universally understood graphic signs and symbols. They ease and ensure speed of conveyance of messages which are important for travellers' security and comfort and make travel and service more seamless and rewarding.

Basing on the comprehensive understanding of tourism[1], of interest to tourism are all public information symbols plus those which are specific to the tourism sector. As a consequence, the term "tourism signs and symbols" can also be alternatively replaced by the term "visitor signage" to embrace the categories of same-day visitors and tourists travelling and staying in all public and specifically tourist areas and facilities.

Certainly, tourism signs and symbols or visitor signage go beyond what can commonly be associated with tourist attractions. It is far more than that, and it is not only pictograms, but also badges, arrows and signposts featuring graphic symbols or written messages.

Some signs and symbols have been standardized already, but their application is not universal, some others may need to be standardized but others must not. However, the status of visitor signage should always be clear to tourism planners and developers so that they could make informed choices about their use and development.

The present publication has three main objectives:

- to inform readers of the status of visitor signage worldwide as it comes to light from the activities concerned of countries, tourism destinations and international organizations;

- to give an aid to local and national tourism planners and communication managers in tourism businesses such as tour and transport operators, hotel companies, recreation establishments, etc.

- to encourage tourism educators and trainers to include visitor signage into respective curricula, especially for tourist guides and escorts.

1. SOURCES OF INFORMATION

The findings of the WTO survey on tourism signs and symbols (November 1997-March 1998)[2], given in the interim Report on the Status of Tourism Signs and Symbols Worldwide (QSC.3/2(d)), and an earlier document Report on the Standardization of Tourist Signs and Symbols published by the WTO Secretariat in 1989 (PG(VI)B.5.1)[3], as well documents received from ISO Technical Committee 145 - Public Information Symbols, were mainly used in preparing this publication.

A detailed list of information sources is given in the Bibliography at the end of this publication.

2. LESSONS FROM THE 1997-1998 WTO SURVEY ON TOURISM SIGNS AND SYMBOLS

While tourism signs and symbols may contribute to achieving more transparency in the world of tourism, the WTO survey strengthened the overriding conviction that more information and transparency were urgently needed on how visitor signage can be made and improved and who could take an initiative and assume responsibility for this activity to generate benefits for all.

The WTO survey confirmed that all efforts leading to this objective are valid, but that such efforts should be recognized within the mainstream activities in this area and lead to a worldwide harmonization and possibly standardization.

Harmonization is the core of the methodological approach and criteria to develop standardization of symbols for visitor signage, which has to reply to three requirements:

• Visibility
• Permanence
• Coherence

It is therefore hoped that this publication will help in raising awareness of tourism decision-makers concerned with a view to providing conceptual, material and operational support to the work which stays ahead for a number of years.

3. THE NECESSARY BASIC CONCEPTS

Signs and symbols were humanity's first tools for communication. Semiology (the science that studies signs and symbols within social life) allows to understand how the different uses of signs and symbols are established, for example, for the purposes of tourism[4]. According to the pioneers of semiology[2], the sign should be meaning, that is, it is an active process, the result of a dynamic interaction between sign/symbol, object and subject.

Tourism signs and symbols should express their meaning in the most universal and simple language possible. Signs or symbols are not grasped, understood or explained in the same terms nor according to the same reasoning or based on the same premises, by psycho-analysts, sociologists, people from the world of science or religion. The word "symbol" comes from the Greek word "sum-bolon", a "sign of recognition" - an object cut in two constituting a sign of recognition when the bearers are able to put together the two parts. Symbols are required to act as a bridge, to grasp a reality, which can only be expressed indirectly[3]. This is the reason why the notion of the symbol may be very imprecise and may give rise to acceptations that are sometimes contradictory[4].

A symbol is an "object or natural fact in the form of an image which leads, by its shape or nature, to an association of natural ideas (within a given social group) with something abstract or absent"[5]. It is therefore conceived as a mediator[6]; it is the visible face of the invisible, the expression of the element that gives rise to an expression.

When the semiologists showed the difference between the signifier and the signified, they pointed out that signs/symbols could be the object of disjunction. But it is the art of conjunction that must be emphasized by the tourism sign or symbol, as the meeting between cultures and societies, which are often very different[7]. Within the framework of the tourism phenomenon, "signs and symbols" should form part of non-written communication, which is more universal than language and languages, even languages that are very widely spoken in the international travel and tourism sector such as English. However, the development of certain communication techniques moulds our senses and cognitive processes so that it becomes impossible to separate thought content and the form of expression transmitting the though. Other contemporary thinkers such as Regis Debray[8] consider that civilizations pass through three stages: the logosphere (the spoken word), the graphosphere (the written word), and the videosphere (images or signs and symbols) in which we live today.

Research into signs and symbols necessarily has to involve not only semiology but also other disciplines such as:

- Linguistics. Tourism signs and symbols include written information (name of a place or site, distance in kilometres, etc.) which may be given in a language that is read in a different way to the tourist's language (from right to left or from top to bottom instead of from left to right). And the meaning of a written sign may even vary amongst people having the same language (Chinese or even Spanish as spoken in Europe or Latin America).

- Psycho-sociology. The individual or collective approach to a symbol may vary according to certain elements of the psychological and social environment.

- Law and jurisprudence. There may be legal implications in the creation and widespread adoption of signs and symbols (such as those aiming to facilitate movement or to reduce barriers to travel and tourist flows).

- Aesthetics and environment. Account must be taken of the aesthetic effects of producing signs and symbols on subjectivity and the construction of meaning in the cultural environment and natural landscape.

- Economics and regional development.

In an increasingly complex world that contains a great diversity of societies and cultures, signs need to be heterogeneous but not disparate. Tourist signs or symbols cannot have a hidden sense based on a special code that can only be deciphered by people trained in it or who have had access to it. The person for whom the sign is intended (tourist or resident) should at least be able to determine the preliminary conjectures of the sign or symbol, amongst them the real intentions of the person who issued the sign and the cultural framework to which the message belongs.

The physical environment of the sign or symbol is important to interpretation. A signpost in an area of sand dunes will be easier to understand and interpret if it bears a symbol showing that a spring or an oasis is close by than if it points the way to Paris 5,000 km away. This in no way affects the authenticity of the physical or cultural environment. Signs do not trivialize a tourist attraction or detract from its prestige or its exclusive nature. They merely place it within a universal system of communication. They allow for translation into a language that can be understood by the majority.

THE NEED FOR ROAD SIGNAGE FOR TOURISM

Road signage for tourism turns out to be inappropriate and insufficient, especially in rural areas, although sometimes there may be even too many in the most popular places, thus creating confusion and visual pollution. The national and local tourism administration should have a determined policy for straighten it out.

Tourism development plans should cover road signs to allow domestic and foreign visitors to receive information on the location of sites or attractions and/or how to reach them.

In order to achieve this objective, the tourism administration should proceed step by step:

- to define in advance any sites and places worth visiting, starting with those on the tourist circuits and determining the most suitable locations for signposts;
- as appropriate, to reach an agreement with the Ministry responsible for roads and/or transport:
- to define with this Ministry the criteria for installing general road signs in the characters of the national alphabet or in Latin characters or by figures (numbers, road numbers, distances to towns and villages, junctions, etc.);
- to choose the symbols to be adopted, first using signs and symbols that are internationally accepted or widely used;
- to replace, in agreement with the appropriate local authorities, any existing signs to bring them into line with national and international standards;
- to define associated projects such as rest areas, panoramas and viewpoints and equip them with appropriate signs.

4. A SHORT HISTORY OF VISITOR SIGNAGE

Some historians suggest that signs are an offshoot of printing. It was a printer from Lyon, Charles Estienne, who in 1552 published the first cartographic guides of France ("Le guide des chemins de France" and "les Fleuves au Royaume de France") and invented keys and abbreviations, giving remarkably precise minimal indications on the towns along the routes, the distances between them, the fords, etc. Signs and signals developed naturally with the development of industrial societies and the rise in the surface transport by road and rail. Before, generally, on the roads, local authorities levied a toll and the toll-collector acted as a guide. "He indicated the best routes, where the bridges and fords were, the names of any villages and towns. He also acted as customs agent, foreign exchange broker and could afford safe-conducts"[9].

The first public information symbols in tourist facilities appeared with the development of railways and the construction of large railway stations. Until the years 1840-1850 engines travelled with no visual signals and announced their arrival with whistles or sirens but gradually their increasing speed meant that these methods had to change. The first fixed signal was erected in 1834 on the Manchester to Liverpool line. After 1850, the signaling codes started to be unified according to four main categories that came to be the basis for today's road signs:

- Indications
- Warnings
- Signs to slow down
- Signs to stop

With respect to colours, it was generally accepted that **white** meant "go ahead", **yellow** "slow down" and **red** "stop".
Visitor signage boomed with industrial societies. It was the First World War that speeded up the installation of road signs along the main strategic routes. With the start of mass travel, signage appeared everywhere at the same time as the classification of roads and tourist facilities such as hotels, inns, restaurants, etc.

Today, tourism and visitor signage should be part of tourism policies on information, promotion and regional development, with special emphasis on signposting. A country such as France has created a new word for such activity: "signalétique" i.e. the technique of transmitting tourist information by non-written communication. This tool is developing fast.

In the same time, various tourist satisfaction surveys elaborated in the framework of integrated quality management of tourist destinations showed, from a dual "importance/dissatisfaction", that visitor signage may be a main area of dysfunction in facilities, planning and services of the resorts, especially for "signs for activities" and "direction signposts".

Visitor signage and tourist satisfaction

Since 1993, beach resorts in France have been taking part with the support of the French Agency for Tourism Engineering (AFIT), in a plan to improve resort quality. A survey has been issued to 11,500 tourists presenting the method and the first actions taken by the resorts. The AFIT hopes that the interested parties will endeavour to achieve modern, competitive tourism standards. The surveys carried out during the summer of 1994 (August and September) in 13 beach resorts pointed to the factors that are of importance for tourists:

* Signs for activities (77% importance and 18% dissatisfaction)
* Direction signposts (82% importance and 1% dissatisfaction
* Precision of information received (51% importance and 8% dissatisfaction)

The most critical customers appear to be mostly young, French and staying in commercial accommodation.

This should lead to the adaptation of signs for beaches and ports to prevent overcrowding in certain areas. In addition, arrangements for people with reduced mobility and the study of signposting were done to improve customer flows.

Visitor signage in natural reserves

For natural reserves, very important separate efforts have been made. A guide for visitor signage of France was published in April 1987 by the Ministry of the Environment and the Standing Conference on Natural Reserves. Another guide was published by the same Ministry together with the Natural Area Division of the Department for Nature Protection. The former aimed to be a technical operational tool for rangers includes technical procedures and recommendations. The latter has two sections giving information on signs - the first covers sign design and the second establishes the weak and strong points of all the materials and techniques available with examples (photographs) of signs.

Visitor signage and deregulation

In the United Kingdom, special efforts have been made since 1984, when all signs and symbols were considered to be advertising and were included under the Regulations for advertising in the framework of territorial planning. Tourist surveys showed that signposting played a key role in the choice of site, monument or attraction. When deregulation of signs took place in January 1996, the changes did not have positive consequences- proliferation of signs spoiling the environment, signs with unclear meanings, lack of quality criteria, etc. So to fill the vacuum created by deregulation, the British Standards Institution (BSI) proposed the creation of about 300 public information symbols based on specifications identified by BSI (334 potential symbols were identified) and drawn up in accordance with the principals laid down in ISO 3461. Designing, testing and approving this visitor signage scheme is expected to cost the equivalent of about 50 million US dollars.

Experience is being gained; every destination and territory is looking for its own identity and uniqueness through a new type of signs, giving rise to batteries of logos, notice boards, posters, trade marks and signposts with a clutter of national and regional messages and incoherence. The search for consistency must therefore be one of the main obligations of those responsible for tourism signs and symbols.

5. APPLICATION

Tourism signs and symbols are mainly found in:

- public places such as airports, seaports, bus and railways stations and terminals, etc.

- roads, streets, paths, trails, ski slopes, etc.

- buildings,

as well as maps, orientations diagrams, guidebooks and tourism pamphlets, and now more and more on Internet portals and web sites (icons).

The status report and guidebook is directed mainly to government officials and private sector professionals who wish to improve visitor signage in their destinations as well as for educators, tourism guides and escorts who wish to have a better knowledge on this subject.

Comments and examples are welcome by WTO so that it can continue to work to improve the quality of tourism and fulfil the Organization's role as a clearing house in this important area.

[1] "the activities of persons travelling to and staying in places outside their usual environment for not more than one consecutive year for leisure, business and other purposes". See Recommendations on Tourism Statistics, United Nations/World Tourism Organization, UN Series M, No.83, New York 1994.

[2] To which over fifty countries and territories contributed information and ideas

[3] See Annex 1 of the present publication.

[4] From the historical past, graphic symbols in the form of logotypes have survived in shields, blazons, coats of arms as well as flags and banners symbolising lineage and historical families. They can still be found on buildings and in tourist guides. Some coats of arms and colours have developed into national symbols.

2 Especially Ferdinand de Saussure.

[3] cf. Charles Morris, Foundations of a theory of signs, Chicago UP, Chicago, 1938.

[4] The first semiologists made a distinction between three types of sign: indications, icons and symbols. As explained in "Main terms used", the indication is a sign that relates to the material object (smoke indicates fire, movement of the weather vane indicates wind, etc.). The icon is a sign creating an analogy and resemblance with the object in question. This is why icons were chosen to facilitate computing tasks. Finally, the symbol sets itself apart to reinforce its functionality and efficiency.

[5] Petit Dictionnaire Robert, Paris,1999.

6 According to philosopher Paul Ricoeur.

[7] See especially Umberto Eco, I limiti dell'interpretazione, Di Fabbri, Milan, 1990.

[8] Régis Debray, Manifestes médiologiques, Paris, Gallimard, 1994.

[9] See Marc Boyer and Philippe Viallon in La communication touristique, PUF, Paris, 1994.

CHAPTER I

NATIONAL EXPERIENCES IN THE FIELD OF TOURISM SIGNS AND SYMBOLS

The countries which in recent years have dealt with tourism signs and symbols, have sought to apply the principles of uniformity, consistency and continuity, and this involves better-defined procedures between local and national levels.

Policies on tourism signs and symbols are usually drawn up on a national level and the more developed the tourism industry in a country or territory, the more likely it is that there will be a coherent, centralized and coordinated policy in line with the international agreements and regulations.

The countries and territories may adopt specific rules and regulations governing tourism signs and symbols on a national scale and for the whole of the national territory, as part of general rules and regulations applicable to all sectors. This situation is found mainly in Europe. But it tends to be known in other continents, especially in countries intending to put in place or reinforce a comprehensive national policy[1].

Such policy supported by laws and regulations can be applied to the different types of signs and symbols according to the following categories[2]:

A. Public information symbols in tourist facilities

B. Public information symbols at tourist sites

C. Road signs

D. Signs in bus and railway stations, seaports and airports

E. Symbols for tourist facilities

F. Symbols for tourist attractions

G. Tourist routes (markers)

H. The official "tourist information" sign

I. The national tourism promotion logo

1. ROLE OF NATIONAL TOURISM ADMINISTRATIONS AND OFFICES

In more and more countries and territories, the National Tourism Administrations and Offices bear responsibility on a national level for the adoption and implementation of tourism signs and symbols. If not, they are consulted in this matter by another competent body.

Who bears responsibility for visitor signage?

In the Republic of Cyprus, the Ministry of Communication and Public Works consults the Cyprus Tourism Organisation before placing a sign for a specific tourist attraction. In Jordan, the NTA/NTO responsibility is shared with the Royal Jordanian Automobile Club, the Ministry of Public Works and Housing and the Royal Jordanian Geographic Centre; in China, with the national technical administration for supervision and management; in Macao with the Public Works Department; in Romania with the Ministries of the Environment and the Interior.

The responsibility of adopting and implementing visitor signage is also often shared with the municipal and provincial tourism bodies for the public information symbols at tourist sites as in the cases of Bolivia, Peru, Laos, China, Macao, Israel and Romania or with the Tourism & Hotel Association as in Aruba.

LATIN - AMERICAN EXPERIENCES[3]

The Argentinian signs system for tourism

In Argentina, since 1979 the National Tourism Secretariat has set up the National signs system for Tourism with a view to proposing a coherent system for signs in tourism locations. The basic idea behind the system is to replace written language by graphic language, eliminating explanatory texts, adopting uniform type, including urban signs and using the colours that are generally used internationally.

The Bolivian manual on tourism signs

In August 1997 Bolivia published a manual entitled "Methodology for tourism signs" (Department of Planning, National Tourism Secretariat, Ministry of Economic Development, La Paz) which describes the main types and functions of signs; general signs, signs for the movement of persons or vehicles and general information signs, especially for health and communications services. The manual states that the National Tourism Secretariat is responsible for the application on a national level of the methodology proposed. This method has also been validated on both national and sectorial levels by its directive on tourism quality in Bolivia. It was drawn up basing on symbols that have already been adopted and on a full semiotic study and refers to institutions such as the National Roads Department, the Geographic Military Institute and other organizations. The National Roads Department draws up road signs in line with the Inter-American manual of methods for controlling traffic which was prepared in 1964 through the Organization of American States. The manual gives all the technical data (size, colour, symbols, graphic features, etc.) to be taken into account in signs and defines how signs should be erected.

In general, the following are the main issues and topics addressed in visitor signage policies at country or territory levels:

- Elaboration and adoption of rules and regulations
- Rules/regulations applicable at all establishments and activities on:
    - General information and security
    - Attractions and culture
    - Sport and recreation activities
    - Transport modes and terminals
    - Tourist equipment
    - Beach flag warning system
    - Marker colour systems

2. FINANCE OF VISITOR SIGNAGE

National tourism administrations and offices do not appear as the main financial contributors to visitor signage. Local authorities tend to have a more important role. Only a few tourism administrations report to have a separate budget for the planning and installation of a visitor signage system[4].

It is recommended that tourism administrations not only have a budget for implementing visitor signage, but also to test its use and assist local authorities in putting it in place.

With this objective in mind, a visitor signage budget should feature such items as:

- Research and design of signs and symbols (including testing)
- Manufacture of signposts (including boards)
- Installation and maintenance of signposts

A CONTINUOUS HUMAN AND FINANCIAL EFFORT

In Argentina, the National Tourism Secretariat has drawn up a study on the national tourism sign system with a view to proposing a coherent system for signs in tourism locations. The study shows that efforts to standardize signs need to be continuous because signs inevitably evolve over time. A budget must be dedicated to it. The study covers several experiences of provincial official bodies and the Argentine Automobile Club. It states that, since 1979, the Secretariat has been endeavouring to draw up a coherent system of signs ("the National System for Tourism Signs" - Resolution n°4 of the National Conference in San Juan, 10-12 May 1979) and that the system proposed be applied in the capital and in various provincial jurisdictions, namely Misiones, Chubut, Santa Cruz, Santiago de Estero, San Luis, Cordoba. The system has also been proposed to other Latin American countries such as Brazil, Chile, Nicaragua and Venezuela.

3. PARTNERSHIPS

The private sector and its associations are increasingly participating and intervening in a visitor or tourism signage policy and the standardization of some symbols: for example in Lesotho; in Aruba (with the Tourism 8 Hotels Association and the hotel chains); in the Czech Republic (with the Czech Tourism Club Green-ways for cycling, ski and walking trails); in Finland (with the Holiday Farms Association). In Portugal professional associations are consulted so as to follow the best and more consensual procedures.

More important however, is the role to be played by National Standards Organizations or Associations. Austria indicates, for example, that agreements on all tourism signs and symbols (except for those that are standardized by law) must be reached with the Austrian Standards Institute (a private association which has as members of its Supervisory Committee the Federal Ministry of Economic Affairs and the Federal Chamber of Economy).

In the last few years, as far as possible, National Tourism Administrations or Offices report to have found it necessary to contribute towards a visitor signage policy, within the existing regulatory framework, in partnership with:

- ISO member associations such as AENOR in Spain, AFNOR in France, BSI in the United Kingdom, ANSI in the United States of America, SAA (Standards Australia), SCC (Standard Council of Canada) or SNZ (Standards New Zealand),

- other governmental bodies and organizations in charge of roads, airports and other transportation systems, national and regional parks, security, etc.,

- local and regional tourist or community authorities,

- representative travel trade associations.

EXAMPLES

Guidelines for tourism signs: A Publication of the Western Australian Tourism Commission[5]

The Western Australian Tourism Commission is a regional authority in charge of tourism in Western Australia. In June 1995, the Commission with some assistance of Main Roads Western Australia, the regional body in charge of road traffic, published a short handbook entitled "Guidelines for Tourism Signs" to:

- provide a better understanding of existing signage policies and standards,
- identify who is responsible for their provision and maintenance,
- determine what is necessary to meet the needs of visitors,
- assist those who are interested in safety directing the road users' attention to tourist attractions or service facilities,
- attempt to limit the size, clutter and inefficiency of uncontrolled and inappropriate signs, which create aesthetic and safety problems, whilst encouraging more effective signs through the adoption of a uniform approach to signage throughout the State, etc.

Among the key policy guidelines, the document underlines that:

- Signs should not be used as the primary means of identification. Good road and tourist maps are always recommended to be used as the primary means of locating tourist attractions and services. Road signs then become a means of reinforcing their precise location and reassuring motorists that they are travelling in the right direction.
- Local government authorities and tourist centres are encouraged to develop and implement a regular and systematic inspection programme and to maintain an up-to-date inventory for their area.

COLOURS

The Western Australia Guide reminds that:

- Regulatory signs usually contain an element in red

- Warning signs are usually black on yellow background

- Guide signs are white on green background

- Service signs are on white on blue background

- Tourism signs are white on brown background

The guide also calls the attention of those responsible for tourism sign-posting to important related issues by providing lists of:

- service benefits on road reserve environment (footpaths and cycle-ways, public utilities, traffic signs and directional signs, parking, rest and picnic areas, information bays),

- environmental benefits of a good advertising management such as the conservation corridors (to protect fauna and native vegetation) and the enhancement of scenic views,

- management issues

- safety aspects such as:

  - Unauthorized signs can detract from the message of legitimate signing,

  - Signs can be badly positioned so that they obstruct or form a confusing background to traffic signs and signals,

- Poor methods of construction and selection of materials can cause dangers to road users and pedestrians,

- Road users can be distracted by inappropriate displays, lightning or positioning of signs,

- Too many signs in one location can also be hazardous to road safety simply because there is too much information for the driver to take in.[6]

In the latter respect, Main Roads Western Australia supplemented the guide with a four-page publication *A guide of roadside advertising* containing principles and tools for roadside advertising:

"The legislation, together with Main Roads guidelines, is designed to work with local Government by-laws to ensure that outdoor advertising does not interfere with the safety of road-users, and to prevent visual pollution".

Peru: A manual on Tourism Signage

In Peru, in 1989 a Manual on Tourism Signs was approved by a ministerial resolution[7] and subsequently published for the purposes of tourism signposting. It includes the main tourism signs to be used on roads and in urban centres, and provide guidance on the design procedures for symbols setting. Only two series of referents are included under standardized tourism symbols: for accommodation establishments and for restaurants.

In addition, the manual explains that:

- the Ministry of Transport, Communication, Habitat and Construction is in charge of symbols relating to civil aviation, roads and transportation systems,
- the National institute of Civil Defense is in charge of symbols relating to safety with regard to earthquakes and other natural disasters,
- the National Institute for Natural Resources and the National Institute for Culture adopt signs and symbols for the use of National Natural and Cultural Heritage Areas.

China: "Graphic signs for tourist hotels" and "Graphical symbols for use on public information signs"

The People's Republic of China has published two brochures for national and international purposes on the above subjects where a series of symbols are presented.

The brochure whose title in English is "Graphic signs for tourist hotels" LB/T001-1995 was published in 1995 in Chinese and English and lists the standards and corresponding pictograms and some explanations in Chinese for the industry. It contains two types of symbols: for hotel services and features and for general public information:

A1	Taxi	ISO 7001: 1990(012)
A2	Parking for bicycle	ISO 7001: 1990(023)
A3	Rubbish receptacle	ISO 7001: 1990(018)
A4	Guard	
A5	Emergency call	
A6	Emergency signal	
A7	Fire alarm	
A8	Fire extinguisher	ISO 7001: 1990(014)
A9	Direction	ISO 7001: 1990(001)
A10	Way in	ISO 7001: 1990(026)
A11	Way out	ISO 7001: 1990(027)
A12	Emergency Exit	
A13	Stairs	ISO 7001: 1990(013)
A14	Stairs up	
A15	Stairs down	
A16	Escalator	
A17	Elevator; lift	ISO 7001: 1990(021)
A18	Facilities for disabled person	
A19	Toilet	ISO 7001: 1990(006)
A20	Toilet male; man	
A21	Toilet female; woman	
A22	Men's locker	
A23	Women's locker	
A24	Drinking water	
A25	Mailbox	
A26	Postal service	

A27	Telephone	ISO 7001: 1990(008)
A28	Check-in; reception	
A29	Information	
A30	Currency exchange	ISO 7001: 1990(020)
A31	Settle accounts	
A32	Lost and found; lost property	ISO 7001: 1990(049)
A33	Left luggage	ISO 7001: 1990(028)
A34	Luggage trolley	
A35	Laundry	
A36	Drying	
A37	Ironing	
A38	Barber	
A39	Restaurant	ISO 7001: 1990(031)
A40	Chinese restaurant	
A41	Snack Bar	
A42	Bar	
A43	Coffee	
A44	Flower	
A45	Book and newspaper	
A46	Conference room	
A47	Dance Hall	
A48	OK, karaoke bar	
A49	Cinema	
A50	Sauna	
A51	Massage	
A52	Swimming	
A53	Chess and cards	
A54	Table tennis	
A55	Billiards	
A56	Bowling	
A57	Golf	
A58	Squash/Racquet ball	
A59	Tennis	
A60	Gymnasium	
A61	Sporting activities	ISO 7001: 1990(029)
A62	Silence	
A63	Smoking allowed	ISO 7001: 1990(002)
A64	Smoking not allowed	

Comment: *Many symbols are on line with ISO standards (ISO Standard 7001).*

The brochure entitled "Graphical symbols for use on public information signs" (GB 10001-94) presents 79 signs which are used as standardized symbols in China. Many of these symbols are found in the previous document ("Graphic signs for tourist hotels").

France: A guidebook on tourist signage "A guide for your use"[8]

The French Ministry of Tourism and the Ministry of Equipment, Housing and Transportation published in 1992 a guide on Visitor and Tourist Signage ("Signalétique"). The main feature of this guide is a list of all the resources available for both road signs and advertising with a view to protecting the natural and cultural heritage as well as road safety.

The Guide is intended for "decision-makers in various fields of tourism ... who are keen to improve the historic and natural service and leisure potential of our country".

"With the assistance of technicians and specialists, they will be able to organize highway information both to satisfy visitors and to develop a common purpose and synergy between inhabitants and socio-professional groups to enhance the value of our diversity."

The Guide explains that, whatever the challenges, the tourist communication policy should be based on two vehicles:

1. **Promotion:** its role is to create a motivation, establish or develop a tourism activity and to stimulate, and thus guide, the desire to travel and discover. Signage is one of its tools.

2. **Highway communication**: its role, once an interest has been aroused, is to enable everyone to reach the desired destination simply and pleasantly.

The communication policy is based on several regulatory texts, the main ones being the amended ministerial order of 24 November 1967 concerning road and motorway signs and the inter-ministerial instruction on road signs.

THE COMPONENTS OF THE FRENCH ROAD SIGNAGE

1.   DIRECTION INDICATORS
2.   INFORMATION SIGNS
3.   LOCATION INDICATORS
4.   SIGNS INDICATING ENTRY INTO AND
      EXIT FROM BUILT-UP AREAS
5.   INFO STATIONS OR INFORMATION BAYS
6.   CULTURAL AND TOURISM
      INFORMATION SIGNS
7.   SIGNS INDICATING
      MOTORWAY RECREATION AREAS
8.   TOURIST ROUTE SIGNS
9.   IDEOGRAMS (SYMBOLS)

Source: Signalisation touristique: Guide, Paris, mars 1992

The Guide also gives very precise indications on the conditions for use of road signage, their employment in signage development plans (in area and urban development plans), the rules for the use of certain EU-type (European Union) entry signs for administrative regions or departments and signs depicting urban limits.

Signage development plans are now the indispensable tools for urban and area planning and development. They reply to the question: *WHAT SHOULD BE SIGNPOSTED?* They should be studied globally and not during the introduction of the signs.

The Guide describes in particular the Info Stations or Information Bays (RIS – Network of Info Stations). These are small facilities, sometimes a solid building, bordering the motorway or tourist route providing clear, explanatory signs and often toilets. A guide to this effect was published in January 19859. It was produced to meet such tourist needs as:

- reception in a geographical area
- information concerning a tourist zone
- information on generic terms
- information indicating a change on a main highway or built-up area
- information on accommodation facilities
- information on tourist routes
- information concerning famous personages
- information on regional products

Lastly, the guide sets out general principles on outside advertising in tourism areas (hoarding, billboards, advertising signs at ground level, luminous slide advertisements, small signposts and street furniture). It advises local partners, advertisers, and poster advertising companies to incorporate signs into the landscape in such a way that they do not detract from its aesthetic quality (control of visual pollution).

The Spanish system of endorsed tourism signage (SISTHO)

The Spanish constitutional system has granted the main competencies on tourism to the Autonomous Communities, except on national matters. An interministerial cooperation has been established between the Secretariat of State for Trade, Tourism and SME of the Ministry of Economy and Finance, and the Secretariat of State for Infrastructure and Transport of the Ministry for Development, in order to open the way for the harmonization of visitor signage at the national levels.

An agreement was signed between both administrations on 19 September 1998 with the purpose of establishing a visitor signage system aimed to inform people who travel on national roads and highways leading to special tourist interest destinations. Furthermore, the modernization of visitor signage meant to stimulate the adoption of a system accepted by the Autonomous Communities. Among the actions contemplated in the agreement there are three main objectives:

1. Selection of especially prominent tourist destinations ("superdestinos"): so far, 318 destinations considered important for signage have been determined (June 1999).

2. Endorsement of a design method according to normal procedures in the field of road signage as for dimensions, colour, reflectance, graphs, letter types, general location, etc. with designs corresponding to three categories in which the tourist destinations have been grouped in a first stage: - nature, – cultural–artistic, - sun and beach and special tourist destinations in a second stage.

3. Preparation of road signage standards for an endorsed tourist information system, in which criteria have been set for the location of postsigns, materials to be used, installation and construction, etc. These criteria must ensure a correct perception of the message inside parameters of quality assurance and road safety, the avoidance of interference with other signs and symbols, maintenance and conservation, etc.

In the framework of SISTHO, a possibility is given to signal other tourist destinations of difficult classification, but of growing importance, such as tourist routes, sport activities (ski stations, marinas, golf courses, wind-surfing, motor- racing circuits, sport aviation, horse ways, etc.) and thematic parks.

One of the most arduous problems of the system was to determine how to qualify the tourist destinations worthy of being signaled. Four well-known tourist guides such as "Anaya", "Michelin", "Spain under the Sun" and "El Pais" are used for the evaluation of the tourist site. The destinations have been assessed as a whole and not for all of their attractions. A catalogue of endorsed tourist signs and symbols (CATHO) was implemented during the year 2000 by the General Directorate of Roads and Highways.

P. Clave:
CULTURA

P. Clave:
NATURALEZA

P. Clave:
SOL Y PLAYA

Source: Ministerio de Fomento and Globalesco, Madrid, 1999, Pictogramas - C

Type of symbol: Road orientation signs
Background colour: Brown (following UE rule)
Composition: Matrix type S-224 including pictogram
Pictograms: Polychromic (better quality perception)

United Kingdom: symbols for tourist guides, maps and countryside recreation[10]

This booklet, last revised and updated in 1993, was intended for the use of publishers of guidebooks, maps and other publications directed at providing information for tourists. After an introduction, the different chapters of the booklet:

- Give examples of symbols shown in use

- Illustrate symbols, which may be used in the preparation of tourist publications and accommodation guides

- Illustrate some additional symbols for specialist use

- Illustrate symbols to help people with disabilities

- Contain symbols specifically for use in the countryside

- Contain symbols for signposting tourist attractions on roads.

The sponsoring organizations connected with this publication support the work of the committees working under the auspices of the International Organization for Standardization (ISO) towards standardization of public information symbols and the efforts made by the European Union and trade bodies within the EU to introduce wider harmonization of symbols. The booklet is available in DTP format for an easy reprint of symbols. Almost 500 symbols are illustrated.

All the symbols are displayed in alphabetical order and are classified in six categories appropriate to their use in commercial or local guidebooks:

- Camping and caravan parks

- Holiday camps, chalet parks, etc.

- Serviced accommodation

- Self-catering accommodation

- Recreational and sports facilities

- Tourist facilities

- Suitable for maps and diagrams

With respect to variants, publishers may wish to use a symbol for differing but related subjects (the exact wording used can even be altered for individual purposes). The booklet proposes referents to symbols and does not forbid graphical variants. It is also possible to use symbols at different angles.

4. CONFIRMED STATUS OF THE USE OF SOME SIGNS AND SYMBOLS (ACCORDING TO THE WTO SURVEY OF 1998)

SAFETY SYMBOLS

Countries and territories[11] mentioned below report having standardized safety symbols for their internal use. However, such symbols, among the first subject to standardization at national level, appear not to be always harmonized internationally.

Fire escapes: Lesotho, Morocco; Argentina, Aruba, Bolivia, Ecuador, México; Macao; Austria, Cyprus, Czech Republic, Finland, Israel, Italy, Portugal, Romania, Slovakia, the Former Yugoslav Republic of Macedonia (FYROM); Turkey; Jordan.

Fire: Lesotho, Morocco; Argentina, Aruba, Bolivia; Austria, Cyprus, Czech Republic, Finland, Israel, Italy, Portugal, Romania, Slovakia, the Former Yugoslav Republic of Macedonia (FYROM); Turkey; Jordan.

Emergency exit: Malawi, Morocco; Argentina, Aruba, Bolivia, Ecuador; Macao; Austria, Czech Republic, Finland, Israel, Italy, Portugal, Romania, Slovakia, the Former Yugoslav Republic of Macedonia (FYROM); Turkey, Jordan; Sri Lanka.

Emergency lighting: Lesotho, Malawi, Morocco; Argentina, Aruba; Macao; Austria, Cyprus, Czech Republic, Finland, Israel, Italy, Portugal, Romania, Slovakia, the Former Yugoslav Republic of Macedonia (FYROM); Turkey, Jordan.

First aid: Lesotho, Morocco; Argentina, Aruba, Bolivia, México; Macao; Austria, Cyprus, Czech Republic, Finland, Israel, Italy, Portugal, Romania, Slovakia, the Former Yugoslav Republic of Macedonia (FYROM); Turkey, Jordan; Sri Lanka.

First aid stations: Morocco; Argentina, Bolivia, Ecuador; Macao; Austria, Cyprus, Israel, Italy, Portugal, Slovakia, the Former Yugoslav Republic of Macedonia (FYROM); Turkey, Jordan; Sri Lanka.

Life buoys (on boats): Morocco; Argentina, Ecuador; Cyprus, Czech Republic, Finland, Israel, Italy, Portugal, Romania, Slovakia; Jordan.

Stretchers: Malawi, Morocco; Argentina; Macao; Czech Republic, Italy, Portugal, Romania.

A fire extinguisher symbol is confirmed in Mexico.

A flashlight on boats symbol is confirmed in Finland.

SYMBOLS FOR PEOPLE WITH DISABILITIES

The 1998 WTO survey identified the countries and territories that have standardized the use of signs and symbols to idicate the status of facilities and services with respect to their use by people with disabilities. Annex 5 gives examples of such symbols and their variants.

Entrances, interiors and rooms that are accessible for wheelchairs: Lesotho; Argentina, México; Macao; Cyprus, Czech Republic, Finland, Israel, Italy, Portugal, Romania, Slovakia, the Former Yugoslav Republic of Macedonia (FYROM); Turkey; Jordan.

Accessible lifts: Lesotho, Malawi, South Africa; Argentina, Aruba; China, Laos, Macao; Austria, Cyprus, Czech Republic, Finland (partial), Israel, Italy, Portugal, Romania, Slovakia, the Former Yugoslav Republic of Macedonia (FYROM), Turkey; Iraq, Jordan; Maldives, Sri Lanka.

Spacious or suitable toilets/bathrooms: Lesotho, Malawi, South Africa; Argentina, Aruba, México; China, Laos, Macao; Austria, Cyprus, Czech Republic, Finland, Israel, Italy, Portugal, Romania, Slovakia, the Former Yugoslav Republic of Macedonia (FYROM); Turkey; Iraq, Jordan; Maldives, Sri Lanka.

Accessible telephones: Lesotho, Malawi, South Africa; Argentina, Aruba; China, Laos, Macao; Austria, Cyprus, Czech Republic, Finland, Israel, Italy, Romania, Slovakia, the Former Yugoslav Republic of Macedonia (FYROM); Turkey; Iraq, Jordan; Maldives, Sri Lanka.

Touch systems (Braille): Lesotho.

Ramps: Argentina, Ecuador, México; Macao; Cyprus, Czech Republic, Finland, Portugal, Romania, Slovakia, Turkey; Jordan.

Car parking places for people with limited mobility: Lesotho; Argentina, México; Macao; Cyprus, Czech Republic, Finland, Portugal, Romania, Slovakia; Turkey; Jordan.

CODE COLOURS FOR BEACH WARNING FLAGS

With regard to beach safety, which is found of vital importance in leisure tourism, the International Federation of Tour Operators (IFTO) took the initiative in early 1997 of collecting information on the use of beach warning flags in different countries. WTO and APEC were also asking countries and territories on the colours used to indicate the status of bathing water (beach safety).

The results of the IFTO survey were as follows:

- Anguilla: no flag warning system
- Antigua & Barbuda: no flag warning system
- Australia (Queensland): green for safety, yellow for caution, red for danger
- Barbados: green for safety, yellow for caution, red for danger
- Canada: no flag warning system
- Cayman Islands: no flag warning system
- Cyprus: red for danger
- Dubai: white for safety, red for danger
- Florida: no flag for safety, yellow for caution, red for danger
- France: green for safety, orange for caution, red for danger
- Gambia: white for safety, red for danger
- Gibraltar: green for safety, yellow for caution, red for danger
- Grenada: no flag warning system
- Hong Kong: red/yellow indicates lifeguards are present, red for danger, blue on white indicates report of shark in the vicinity
- India - Goa: green for safety, red for caution, black for danger
- Ireland: red on yellow for safety, red for danger
- Italy: no flag for safety, yellow for caution, red for danger
- Jersey: red/yellow for safety, red for danger
- Malta: no flag warning system
- Mauritius: no flag warning system
- Monaco: green for safety, orange for caution, red for danger
- Morocco: white for safety, orange for caution, red for danger
- Philippines: no flag warning system
- Portugal: green for safety, yellow for caution, red for danger
- Seychelles: red/yellow for safety and caution, red for danger
- Singapore: no flag warning system

- South Africa: green for safety, yellow for caution, red for danger
- Spain: green for safety, yellow for caution, red for danger
- St. Kitts: no flag warning system
- St Vincent and the Grenadines: no flag warning system
- Tunisia: white for safety, orange for caution, red for danger
- United Kingdom: green for safety, orange for caution, red for danger

In supplementing this information, the WTO survey identified the following use of colours:

(a) For safe bathing
- white in Morocco, Mexico, Israel, Slovakia
- light blue in Argentina
- green in Macao, Cyprus, Finland, Portugal, Sri Lanka

(b) For bathing with caution
- red in Morocco, Israel, Romania
- yellow/black in Argentina
- yellow in Ecuador, Mexico, Macao, Cyprus, Finland, Portugal, Slovakia
- no flag in Sri Lanka

(c) For danger, bathing not permitted
- black in Morocco, Israel, Romania, Slovakia
- red and black in Argentina
- red in Ecuador, Mexico, Macao, Cyprus, Finland, Italy, Portugal, Sri Lanka.

In addition, **APEC** provided the following data on the use of the beach flag warning system among its member economies:

Australia:	yellow or red for Care needed, and red for Do not swim
Canada:	no colour code
Chile:	green for Safe
Chinese Taipei:	green for Safe, yellow for Care needed, and red for Do not swim

New Zealand: yellow and red flags are used to indicate the area patrolled by lifeguards. Swimmers are advised to swim between the yellow and red flags. If no flags are displayed the beach is not patrolled.

Thailand: green for Safe and red for Do not swim.

Conclusion: As emphasized by IFTO, the present range of colours is "at best confusing and at worst dangerous", considering the fact that international leisure travellers move from one country to another and are confronted with different warning colours. This area is therefore a clear example where international standardization should be considered as a matter of urgency.

LOGOS, SIGNPOSTING AND MARKINGS FOR TOURIST ROUTES AND TRAILS

Tourist routes (roads, itineraries, etc.) and trails (paths, tracks, ways, etc.) related to outdoor recreation and sports activities (e.g. climbing, walking, hiking, trekking, cycling, canoeing, skiing, etc.) have become a major tourist attraction and, as a matter of necessity, require the intelligent use of logos, signposting and markings (the latter especially by means of colours).

They are needed for a number of reasons: for general information on existing routes and trails; to provide, promote and strengthen their visibility and image; to facilitate user flows; to provide for users' safety and comfort, to protect the natural environment and, in case of their commercial exploitation, where appropriate, to equip their operators with a handy means to facilitate advertising and marketing.

Standardization of the logo is required for tourist routes whether at national or international levels (when such routes cross various countries). While there will be different logos for different routes each expressing the cultural idiom of its own, the way they are depicted or posted, however, should be subject to international standardization.

Designation of trails for outdoor activities is partly covered by the existing graphic symbols standardized by ISO (see Chapter III) and there appears to be no international standardization for markings. This should be considered seriously for the main reason of safety.

According to the WTO survey, the authorities and other bodies which are competent for the designation, marking, development and maintenance of routes and trails, in which logos, signposting and markings have to be dealt with, vary greatly from one country or territory to another. They can include the NTA or Ministry responsible for tourism (a minority situation) and often another government department (e.g. the Ministry of Transport or Public Works, especially if they are responsible for roads), a national association (such as a sports federation (e.g. for walking and skiing trails, etc.) or provincial or local authorities such as prefectures, town councils and other respective bodies. In some countries, the owners of land may be held responsible for signposting and marking.[12]

Although, as a rule, public funds are used for logo designation, signposting and marking, the private funding and volunteer work can also be employed. An example of the latter is the work accomplished by the French Federation of Hikers[13] which designed, marked and organized about 40,000 km of hiking paths, generally with the help of volunteers and without any official funding.

COLOURS GENERALLY EMPLOYED TO INDICATE TRAILS FOR OUTDOOR ACTIVITIES

For all ski activities and trekking trails as well as climbing, the following colours and signs are generally used[14]:

GREEN FOR EASY AND SAFE

YELLOW OR ORANGE FOR MORE DIFFICULT

RED FOR VERY DIFFICULT

RED AND BLACK FOR DANGER[15]

Concepts developed by France
on routes and trails

Research on routes and trails has been under way in France for about twenty years. Tourist routes stretch from one place to another pass through a certain number of points of interest, are open to visitors, and follow an attractive itinerary[16]. A comprehensive approach is essential to develop quality signposting and to organize and classify itineraries, propose efficient documents on "methods of use" and guarantee quality marking with the help of the RIS (Info – bays network). Any tourist route must be submitted for study by a commission in the "département" or region.

In addition, cultural and tourism promotion on motorways is based on graphic and thematic symbols which aim to break the monotony of motorway driving and give drivers a sense of the location they are passing through by naming the surrounding sights and cultural, tourist and economic assets of the area and indicating any relevant monuments and sights that can be visited and that are close to the main road.

EXAMPLES OF EXISTING ROUTES AND TRAILS [17]

Africa:
- Malawi: Sailing routes on Lake Malawi
- Morocco: Crossing the High Atlas, Imperial Town Circuit, Circuit of Fortified Monuments
- South Africa: Midlands Meander, Wine Route, Kwazulu Natal, and Western Cape

Americas:
- Bolivia: Trekking circuits using the pre-Hispanic routes such as Takesi, Choro, Yunga Cruz, the Gold Route
- Mexico: Mundo Maya, Colonial cities, Barrancas del Cobre, and the route taken by Hernan Cortés

Europe:
- Finland: the King's Road, the Häme Ox Road
- Georgia: the Silk Road (International Route)
- Israel: the great crossing of Israel, regional nature walks, Via Maris (the idea is to restore an old route that went from Egypt to Turkey through Israel)
- Italy: Archaeological walks
- Poland reports 24,643 km of hiking paths, 9,980 km of mountain paths, 324 km of skiing routes in Poland. The International Cycling Route and several hundreds of kilometres of cycling trails have been marked out in Poland. There are also marked paths in the Sudety, Tatra, Beskidy, Bieszczady and Gory Swietokrzyskie Mountains and two canoeing circuits on the Brda and Krutyn rivers.
- Czech Republic: Cycling route from Prague to Vienna (the green route)

COLOUR MARKER SYSTEMS FOR TOURIST ROUTES AND TRAILS

The marker systems used for tourist routes and trails that have been identified are usually colour bands or arrows, for example:

- brown arrows in Lesotho
- blue lines in Malawi
- fluorescent painted bands and arrows in Morocco
- green for roads, blue for cycling and walking paths in Cyprus
- brown symbols and signs in Finland
- colour marks and pictograms at the start of paths in Israel
- white and green in the Czech Republic
- red and blue in Romania
- colour marks in summer and stakes for winter in Slovakia

In Argentina, colours vary according to the type of environment, whether urban, rural, indoor or outdoor.

Visitor signage and the use of bar codes

Bar codes[18] may be originated from the Morse code invented in the 19th century. Although the relationship between bar codes and tourism does not come to be evident, this area must be looked into carefully in view of the new technologies of information intervening in tourism. In essence, bar codes are graphic symbols, but they are read by machines (scanners). In their most common form, linear bar codes are a series of alternating dark and light bars, in various widths, which reflect light within an acceptable reflectance tolerance as prescribed by specifications. Most linear symbols are bi-directional, i.e. the data carrier may be read left – to – right and right – to – left.

They are increasingly used to exchange information on the characteristics of products and services and to improve the accuracy and efficiency of filing and identification by quick electronic scanning[19]. Bar codes are employed for luggage identification in airports or to allow a visitor with a ticket to enter a specific exhibition area or attraction in a museum or a theme park, etc. In the near future, bar codes are very likely to be employed in electronic driving systems to position the driver's location vis-à-vis the destination, a particular site or attraction.

[1] For example, in Argentina tourism signs are included in the National Transit Law that is applicable to the whole industry and its "National system for tourism signs" includes graphic symbols for roads, public transport stops and urban locations as an integral part of an information system for both residents and tourists.

[2] The experience (reflected in the 1997- 1998 survey) suggests that only a few countries and territories have regulations on a regional or local level. Six countries answered in the affirmative: Ecuador, Finland, the Former Yugoslav Republic of Macedonia (FYROM), Lesotho, Mexico and Turkey.

[3] Peru has also published a Manual on tourism signs. It was approved by Ministerial Resolution n° 288-86-ITI/TUR (Ministry of Industry, Foreign Trade, Tourism and Integration, 2nd edition, 1991) and covers design procedures and the main tourism signs on roads and in urban centres. This case is presented further.

[4] Morocco reports to spent the equivalent of US$ 100.000 in 1997. The Visitor Signage system of Jordan was developed with the assistance of USAID for the amount of US$ 125.000.

[5] Western Australian Tourism Commission, June 1995

[6] In the present *Guidelines for Tourism Signs* the types of signs are defined as follows:
Tourist service signs which cover such areas as:
- accommodation facilities
- service stations
- town centres
- local businesses
- sporting venues
- tourist information bays
- tourist information centres
- airports

Tourist Attraction Signs
- national parks
- natural features
- commercial tourist operations
- wineries that cater for tourists
- historic sites and towns
- scenic look-out
- heritage trail

Destination signs (these signs are generally used in conjunction with maps and are considered as reinforcement tools, reassuring motorists that they are travelling in their desired direction)
- advance warning signs
- intersection signs
- fingerboard signs
- position signs
- route marker signs (used for State Tourist Drives)

[7] No 288-86-ITI/TUR, Ministry of Industry, Trade, Tourism and Integration, 2nd edition, 1991.

[8] Ministère du tourisme et Ministère de l'Equipement, du Logement et des Transports, Signalisation touristique: Guide, Direction des Journaux officiels, Paris, mars 1992. In addition, in 1993, the French Ministry of Tourism proposed a graphic chart for multi-lingual information on road signs concerning the French cultural and natural heritage, especially for rural and ecotourism. This graphic chart lays down the dimensions, production specifications, colours and

layout for essential information for visitors in French and in three foreign languages.

[9] Guide relatif aux relais d'information service, Journal Officiel, Paris, janvier 1985.

[10] published by the British Tourist Authority in association with: English Tourist Board, Scottish Tourist Board, Wales Tourist Board, Northern Ireland Tourist Board, Countryside Commission.

[11] The order in which countries and territories are classified follows the regional breakdown employed by WTO (Africa, Americas, Asia and the Pacific, Europe, Middle East, South Asia). The listing is not exhaustive but just a sample derived from 1998 WTO survey.

[12] Some examples of signposting and marking responsibility according to the WTO survey: Malawi, the Lake Malawi Services Company; The Czech Republic, the Czech Tourism Club; Finland, local tourism associations; Israel, the Nature Protection Society; Italy, the owners of land or concession holders with respect to routes and trails; Slovakia: the Slovak Sports Association, the Slovak Tourism Club.

[13] In French, Fédération Française de Randonnée pédestre (FFRP).

[14] In some countries such as Malaysia, the blue is employed for very difficult; in New Zealand, a double black diamond is used for very difficult, a simple black diamond for difficult, a blue square for moderate and a green circle for easy.

[15] Sometimes, it means that the user is asked, before skiing, climbing or touring, to report to patrols.

[16] Guide Signalétique Touristique, France, idem.

[17] In the WTO survey, some countries (e.g. Lesotho, Argentina, China, Macao, Cyprus, Slovakia) indicated having routes and trails, but did not come to identify them. All in all, it is advisable to equip routes and trails with specific identity by using a name or/and a graphic symbol (logo) or both.

[18] The first patent on bar codes was registered in 1952 as a data carrier for commerce and manufacturing.

[19] *"When standardized this global ability can empower international partnerships, drive costs such as relabelling and excess inventory management form the supply chain, increase the responsiveness to customer demand, and accelerate product delivery through the chain."* ISO Bulletin, How bar codes perform: A global primer, August 1997, p. 11.

CHAPTER II

INTERNATIONAL COOPERATION ON PUBLIC AND TOURISM SIGNAGE

International cooperation on transportation signs and symbols of interest to tourism started already before the First World War. Such cooperation is still needed, perhaps more than in the past, due to ever growing movements of people from different cultures and societies, proliferation of tourist routes, competition based on corporate identity, etc. In the past fifty years, two successive trends have emerged:

- Countries and territories follow international conventions, subregional or bilateral agreements[1] to put in place public information symbols or even instruments agreed upon by professional or trade associations (e.g. in the hotel sector[2]). In 1949, a Convention on Road Traffic and a Protocol on Road Signs and Signals were adopted. Their revision was done by the Economic and Social Council of the United Nations (ECOSOC) through its resolutions 967 (XXXVI) of 25 July 1963, 1034 (XXXVII) of 14 August 1964 and 1082B (XXXIX) of July 1965. As a next step, the Convention on Road Signs and Signals was adopted in Vienna in 1968.

- Recently, countries, territories, industry sectors or companies are more keen to invert the process of adopting symbols and standards by following the procedures recommended by the International Organization for Standardization (ISO) through national standardization bodies and technical committees. This trend is fuelled by international agencies such as ICAO, IMO, UIC and lastly WTO and is characterised by public and private sector partnerships.

The main international instrument of interest to tourism is still the Convention on Road Signs and Signals (Vienna, 1968). Efforts of international organizations aimed at harmonizing and standardizing visitor signage need to be sustained[3].

The present WTO action follows on this trend and provides for a number of specific recommendations by taking stock of the prevailing situation and best practices in the field.

1. MAIN INTERNATIONAL INSTRUMENTS FOR VISITOR SIGNAGE

The Convention on Road Signs and Signals

The United Nations Conference on Road Traffic was convened in Vienna at the invitation of the Government of Austria by the Secretary-General of the United Nations in accordance with resolutions 1129 (XLI) and 1203 (LII) adopted by the Economic and Social Council on 27 July 1966 and 26 May 1967.

The Final Act of the Vienna Conference contains Resolution 1129 (XLI) of the Economic and Social Council concerning the Convention on Road Traffic and the Convention on Road Signs and Signals. This last instrument is the first exhaustive tool for standardizing signs and signals which has a direct or indirect relation with tourism. Both Conventions were adopted on 8 November 1968.

The Convention on Road Signs and Signals was revised in 1995 with regard to special instruction signs and service facility signs (E/Conf. 56/17/Rev.1/Amend.1)[4].

Meanwhile, the 1971 European Agreement supplementing the Convention contains provisions on the signs indicating tourist attractions and signs giving directions (for tourism)[5].

The list of 113 signs and signals covered by the Convention is presented in ANNEX 2 of this Guidebook (The standardized signs of the Convention on Road Signs and Signals, Vienna, 1968).

Main recommendations of the Convention specific to tourism

Five recommendations were proposed for the installation and identification of tourism signs:

"1. Prevent multiplication of tourism signs by prohibiting their installation unless they are indisputably useful in order to avoid devaluating them and especially in order to prevent distracting the attention of road users through excessive signposting as their attention should focus above all on signs that are essential for indicating their itinerary and for ensuring traffic safety.

2. *Do not install such signs where there are already a number of signs giving instructions or indications of special importance for traffic safety, in order to ensure that priority is given by users to instructions or indications for their safety or for clarifying their itineraries.*

3. *Only install tourism signs at a reasonably close distance to the places or centers which are to be indicated in order to avoid trivializing signs and the proliferation of signs which are not essential to the choice of itinerary.*

4. *Differentiate clearly between tourism signs and other types or road signs by keeping for them square or rectangular shapes or the shape of an arrow and coloring them, where possible, brown or white or a combination of these two colors, and ensure that the tourism signs covered by the Vienna Convention on road signs are always used instead of other types.*

5. *As soon as possible, replace names on tourism signs by symbols or pictograms and ensure that these symbols are easy to understand for users and, as far as possible, are identical in the different countries".*[6]

Moreover, signs indicating tourist attractions that are different from those figuring in the Convention on road signs and signals must be designed and installed in compliance with the following principles:

• *"Signs for tourist attractions should only be installed where their usefulness is undeniable. Their importance must not be lessened and the attention of road users must not be distracted by the presence of too many signs."*

- *"Since road users must give priority to road regulations and information aiming to ensure safety or clarity, signs for tourist attractions must never be installed in places where there are already several signs giving instructions or indications that are of special importance for traffic safety."*

- *"Tourist attraction signs must only be installed at a reasonably close distance to the places or centres they indicate."*

- *"The brown colour reserved for tourist attraction signs must never be used for other road signs. It is recommended that countries using other colours for tourist attraction signs should replace them gradually with signs having a brown background and white symbols and/or lettering or brown symbols and/or lettering on a light background."*

- *"Any lettering used on tourist attraction signs should, wherever feasible, be replaced by symbols or pictograms so that the signs can be easily understood by foreign road users."*

The Convention on Road Signs and Signals stipulates also that the Contracting Parties shall limit the number of types of Signs adopted to the minimum necessary and form a coherent system (chapter I, art. 4):

a) *all road signs, traffic light signals and road markings installed in their territory shall form a coherent system and shall be designed and placed in such a way as to be easily recognizable;*

(b) *the number of types of sign shall be limited and signs shall be placed only at points where they are deemed useful;*

(c) *danger warning signals shall be installed at a sufficient distance from obstructions to give drivers adequate warning;*

It shall be prohibited:

- *to affix to a sign, to its support or to any other traffic control device anything not related to the purpose of such sign or device; if, however, Contracting Parties or subdivisions thereof authorize a non-profit making association to install informative signs, they may permit the emblem of that association to appear on the sign or on its support provided this does not make it less easy to understand the sign;*

- to install any board, notice, marking or device which might be confused with signs or other traffic control devices, might render them less visible or effective, or might dazzle road-users or distract their attention in a way prejudicial to traffic safety;

- to install on pavements and verges devices or equipment which might unnecessarily obstruct the movement of pedestrians, particularly elderly or disabled persons.

Thereby, for preparing the European Agreement supplementing the Convention, the European Conference of Transport Ministers agreed on the following basic principles for tourism signs.[7]

"Principle of safety: user safety must not be affected by excessive presence of signs along roads. Tourism signs should therefore not be sited where there are already numerous road signs, especially those giving instructions... However, the correct placement of road signs prevents drivers from hesitating about the road to take. This means that tourism signs may amount to a safety element.

"Principle of proximity: signs and signposts must not be installed too far from the sites, monuments or services to which attention is being drawn. If it seems necessary to keep, in some cases, the idea of tourism markers, a tourism direction sign will be sited reasonably close to the place indicated in order to prevent a proliferation of signs. A limited number of exceptions may be allowed to this principle when the place under consideration is considered of essential importance for a whole region or if it is at the end of an itinerary so that drivers need permanent guidance from long before it.

"Principle of specificity: tourism signs should be differentiated, on the one hand, from advertising signs such as trademarks and pre-trademarks and, on the other, from signs regulating road usage."

Recommendation on the "i" sign, official tourist information sign ("i" or "*i*" sign)

The sign "i" or "*i*" sign was recommended by the International Union of Official Tourism Organizations (which preceded WTO) to indicate the location of a tourist information office. It is the first attempt to standardize a tourism symbol by an international tourism body.

At a meeting of IUOTO Regional Commission for Europe held in Amsterdam (Netherlands) on 28 April 1975, it was considered that most European countries had adopted the "i" or "*i*" sign to indicate the location of a tourist information office with a sign conforming to one of the two models given below. The symbol appearing on one of the two signpost models could be used with a directional sign as in examples E.7 and E.8 given in section B of Annex 5 of the Convention on Road Signs and Signals (a blue letter in a white square with blue background).

Most countries have adopted one of the two standard "i" signs (i or *i*) proposed by IUOTO to indicate the location of a tourist information office. Despite the existence of the official tourist information sign and its use, there is no international agreement on its terms of reference, i.e. who can use it, what type of information services it entitles to (especially whether paid or free-of-charge services), whether authorization is needed for its use, etc[8].

The present most popular official tourist information sign variant is when the "i" (or "*i*") sign is accompanied by a question mark. This practice is seen across all regions (including in Europe) and is preferred outside Europe[9], especially where the Latin alphabet is less or not used. In the APEC region, it is contemplated (an APEC TWG proposal) to officially recommend the use of a question mark.

The draft WTO recommendation " considers that the actual status of the sign is not always clear to its current and potential users and beneficiaries and

1. reaffirms said recommendation to use the "i" (or "*i*") sign in order to:

(a) indicate the location of public tourist information offices

(b) indicate all the other places, whether official or private, where tourism information is provided free of charge to the public at large

(c) indicate the availability of tourist information in printed, audiovisual and electronic media

2. recommends to alternatively use in these instances the "i" (or "*i*") sign accompanied by a question mark."

The joint publication of IMO and ICAO on international signs at airports and marine terminals

The Council of the International Civil Aviation Organization (ICAO) published in 1970 (Document 9430) *"a set of standard signs to facilitate the efficient use of airport terminals by travellers and other users"*. This measure was taken to provide guidance to the many airport authorities faced with increasing congestion in terminal buildings and having to modify or extend their facilities. Signs were experimented and used and the new and revised signs were published in 1984 as the second edition of Doc 9430.

In 1987, the attention of the Facilitation Committee of the International Maritime Organization (IMO) was drawn to the ICAO publication Doc 9430. This IMO Committee considered most of the signs contained therein to be suitable for port use and agreed to consult with ICAO with a view to jointly publishing such signs and symbols for both marine and air terminals.

Previously, during the tenth session of the IMO Assembly in November 1977, a new recommended practice indicated:

"For use at marine terminals and on board ships in order to facilitate and expedite international maritime traffic, public authorities should implement, or where the matter does not come within their jurisdiction, recommend to the responsible parties in their country to implement, standardized international signs and symbols developed or accepted by the Organization in cooperation with other appropriate international organizations, are common to all

modes of transport."

In 1993, the ICAO and IMO Councils approved a new edition of Doc 9430 as a joint ICAO/IMO publication to contribute to the uniform and world-wide adoption of the signs at international airports and marine terminals entitled *"International signs to provide guidance to persons at airports and marine terminals"*. It was published in 1995[10].

The ICAO/IMO publication indicates that the number of signs used should be kept to the minimum consistent with the need to provide guidance to the public. Sometimes, authorities may wish to post additional signs. It was not considered appropriate to deal with them through the development of standard international signs, for example signs covered by national building codes or signs designed for the convenience of passengers rather than to facilitate their movement through terminals.

The general principles concerning the use of signs and the list of 42 recommended signs are given in ANNEX 3 (International signs to provide guidance to persons at airports and marine terminals).

The APEC region study on the standardization of symbols for visitor signage[11]

In 1997, the Tourism Working Group of the Asia Pacific Economic Cooperation (APEC) decided to launch a three-stage study aimed to standardize the symbols for visitor signage of tourist facilities, services and transportation in the member economies:
- to gather and identify major visitor signage systems currently used in the member economies and international organizations
- to evaluate existing signage
- to develop a standardized signage strategy (but not to actually design new signage and an implementation plan).

Information was gathered from most of the 21 APEC members economies (Australia; Brunei Darussalam; Canada; Chile; China, Hong Kong SAR; China; Indonesia; Japan; Korea; Malaysia; Mexico; New Zealand; Papua New Guinea; Philippines; Singapore; Chinese

Taipei; Thailand; United States) and (Peru; Russia; Vietnam). 13 replies to the questionnaire were received from: Australia, Canada (Quebec, Saskatchewan and Yukon), Chile, China, Korea, Malaysia, New Zealand, Peru, Singapore, Chinese Taipei, Thailand.

The findings of the APEC study show the need of a tourism and visitor signage policy. The APEC initiative is the first experience of this kind in the region and a common strategy may be easily adopted. There are no main differences in the systems actually used.

This strategy is to support the following:

- *the combination of the current ICAO, IMO, ISO, UIC and WTO, symbol databases, under the management of a single lead body, i.e. the APEC TWG, to provide a single database for the APEC member economies,*

- *the combination of the current APEC member economies standards when they exist to provide in this database symbols and colour markers referents, which have not been internationally standardized,*

- *the guidance on the use of symbols in a tourist/visitor context and their adoption within standards of tourist/visitor interest to be prepared under the patronage of WTO, ISO and other international organizations,*

- *the strategy must be based on the following principles:*
  - *the more a symbol is used, the more familiar it becomes: introducing needless differences confuses the visitor and undermines the effectiveness of symbols,*
  - *tourists/visitors are being faced with a growing number of symbols: the fewer they have to remember the better (ISO Principle).*

At the same time, it is recommended to provide for a gradual development of visitor signage standards while focusing at the beginning on just a few target areas, for example tourist facilities and attractions.

Symbols proposed for APEC referents: A list of symbol and marker referents has been defined. Some are abstract in nature, but they are fairly familiar. Others are new, but quite representative and would seem to offer a better chance of being understood. It must be recognized that as many of the symbols are aimed at international visitors, they may be misunderstood in some member economies and they are let to the judgment of the TWG members to be accepted or not.

It is also intented to avoid confusion between prohibition behaviour and mandatory behaviour. Some of these symbols may be accompanied by a text, such as the name of the monument, the site, the place where the activity is accomplished, etc. It is considered important that the text does not bring confusion to the meaning of the symbol.

Around 270 symbols, broken down by four major groups are proposed to be standardized:

(a) **Public and tourist safety**
(b) **Tourist transportation**
(c) **Tourist attractions and activities**
(d) **Tourist equipment and facilities**

Route, track or trail markers and beach warning systems are included in the third group.

A second implementation phase may take place in conjunction with PATA and WTO to include these suggested steps, such as:

- to create a Special Committee,
- to reach a consensus on the referents to be adopted as standards by APEC TWG,
- to invite WTO, ISO and major travel and tourism associations which are interested in the project to participate in the Visitor Signage Special Committee,
- to publish a guidebook and brochures,
- to publish web pages on Adopted Visitor Signage Standard Referents (adopted drawings with shape and colours) within the APEC site,
- to invite member economies to test some of the adopted referents in their own tourist facilities and attractions according to the characteristics of their tourist products,
- to invite member economies to take the necessary measures to implement the adopted Standard Referents.

EXAMPLE:
THE BLUE FLAG SIGNS

The Blue Flag award is a label given by the Federation for Environmental Education in Europe (FEEE)[12] for improving the quality of coastal destinations. FEEE proposes 12 signs to express criteria for beach management and safety[13]:

- certified clean water
- information and environmental education[14]
- beach cleansing and refuse collection
- controlled beach life saving
- safe and easy access for disabled persons
- first aid
- no free camping
- compliance with sea shore regulations
- drinking water
- sanitary facilities, no cleaners on the sand
- no vehicular access
- no pets

Signs proposed by the Blue Flag

[1] e.g. in Europe, Southern Africa (with SADC), Latin América.

[2] For example, AH&MA in North America.

[3] Including strategic alliances with tourism industry organizations with a view to obtaining a consensus on visitor signage standardization and inviting members of the World Tourism Organization to take part, in conjunction with ISO and other relevant bodies, in the testing procedures for new signs and symbols subject to standardization (see WTO Secretariat proposals of Council recommendations on tourism signs and symbols (QSC 4/7 (b), Annex 1 (e).

[4] With respect to tourism direction signs, three signs were added in 1995:
* **car-sleeper trains:** the direction towards the place where vehicles are loaded onto the trains as well as the direction for loading the vehicle on a train to go through a tunnel.
* **trains:** the direction for loading the vehicle on a train to go through a tunnel.
* **ferry:** the direction to be taken to embark a vehicle on a ferry.
These symbols must in be in a dark colour on a light background.

[5] (Economic Commission for Europe, Inland Transport Committee, Main Working Group on road transport, Working Group on traffic safety) Document dated 5 May 1997 (TRANS/SC.1/295/Rev.3).

6 Chapter I of the Convention.

7 Economic Commission for Europe, Inland transport Committee, Main Working Group for Road Transport, Working Group on Traffic Safety, in its 14th session (11-15 Feb. 1991):

[8] The "i" sign is generally used in tourism offices (national, regional, local), information offices at bus and railway stations, seaports and airports, other public information offices and, in some cases, tourist or commercial establishments. In Finland, requests for use must be made to the Finnish Tourist Office. In Israel, there are no rules governing its use.

9 For example, in Argentina: "When the national tourism signs system was designed and compared with universal symbols, it was noted that the use of a question mark was widespread. In the tourist information symbol, the criterion chosen was that the question mark should incorporate the logotype of the organization that was indicated."

[10] At the same time, UIC (International Union of Railways) compiled a comprehensive list similar to IMO and ICAO symbols with some variants, for example for refreshments, pharmacy, washing facilities, pushchair, babycare, shopping and specific symbols such as cloakroom, ticket validation, underground station, electric shaver point, hand drier and paper towel dispenser.

[11] APEC, TWG 01/98, Singapour 1999.

[12] The logotype of the Blue Flag is presented in Chapter IV.

[13] See WTO/UNEP/FEEE, Awards for improving the coastal environment: the example of the Blue Flag, Madrid, 1996.

[14] The signs shown in bold type are also presented in Chapter III.

2. VISITOR SIGNAGE POLICY AND INTERNATIONAL STANDARDIZATION

A comprehensive approach towards visitor signage

The setting up of a visitor signage policy may be a long process as it must be accepted not only by the central authorities, but by the local and regional communities and the travel and tourist trade associations.

The following graph presents a scheme of a comprehensive approach towards visitor signage. A similar model was developed by the French Ministries of Tourism and of Equipment, Housing and Transport *. At the design level, the symbols may be standardized according to the following attributes (elements): size, lettering, use of common words and terminology, colour, location (height, distance, position on specific objects).

The facilities for which symbols (signs) may be standardized according to the above characteristics are:

- Maps, including road maps;
- Directional signs (arrows or markers towards a destination);
- Location signs for marking the location of a facility or a service.

---

* Ministère du Tourisme et Ministère de l'Équipement, du Logement et des Transports, Signalisation touristique, Guide, Direction des Journaux Officiels, Paris, France, mars 1992.

A COMPREHENSIVE APPROACH TOWARDS VISITOR SIGNAGE

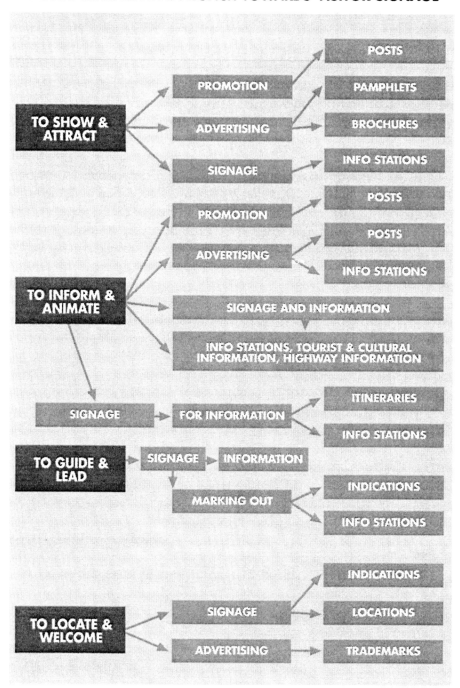

ISO procedures for defining and testing public information symbols (referring also to visitor signage)

A. The standard ISO 7001

One of the main steps in the implementation of a visitor signage policy is to define the function of the symbols to be used and to test them in order to be understood by the largest possible number of people form different cultures and using different languages. Such definitions of functions and testing of comprehensibility were carried out with respect to international standardized referents such as the standard ISO 7001 (international standards for public information symbols)[1] of which fifty-seven referents were adopted until 2000.

The International Organization for Standardization (ISO) is a worldwide federation of national standards bodies (ISO member bodies). The work of preparing international standards is normally carried out through ISO Technical Committees. Draft International Standards adopted by the Technical Committees are circulated to the member bodies for approval before their acceptance as international standards by the ISO Council (with at least 75% approval by the member bodies voting).

ISO has set up a Technical Committee "Graphical symbols"[2] (ISO/TC 145)-Subcommittee SC1(Public information symbols) which aims to standardize the attributes (elements) of graphical symbols, such as their colours in particular, when these elements form part of a message which the symbol aims to represent (for example a safety sign or beach warning sign)[3].

As a result of consultations[4], the WTO Secretariat concluded that **Standard ISO 7001** should be enlarged to 250 to 300 referents, around 40 of them should have testing priority and 160 referents referring to tourist attractions and equipment should be tested with the specific group of users (hotels, tour operators, tourist authorities). Visual design criteria for public information symbols as well graphical symbols covering the needs for information by people with disabilities were also discussed.

B. Other ISO standards affecting directly visitor signage

The basic documents/publications for standardization work include the following:

- ISO/IEC Directives Part 1, "Procedures for the technical work", 3rd edition, 1995 and Amendment 1, 1997-04-15
- ISO/IEC Directives Part 2, "Methodology for the development of further International Standards", 2nd edition, 1992
- ISO/IEC Directives Part 3, "Rules for the structure and drafting of International Standards", 3rd edition, 1997.

Further, ISO /TR 7239 is used to specify a number of definitions and principles (terminology) concerning the development and application of public information symbols, and should be used as a guide to the application of the Standard 7001[5].

ISO 3461: General Principles for Graphical Symbols for use on equipment – Creation of graphical symbols: it provides detailed advice on how to create a symbol, indicating various aspects of graphical design, from orientation to appropriate line thickness.

ISO 3864: 1984 - Colours and safety signals: it provides a system for safety signs where the use of colour and geometric shape are used to identify different categories of use as prohibition signs, mandatory signs, warning signs and information signs concerning safe conditions.

ISO 4196: 1984 - Graphic symbols: use of arrows.

ISO 6309: 1987 - Protection against fire: safety signals.

ISO/TR 7239: 1984 - Development and principles for the application of pictograms: it provides a comprehensive procedure which emphasizes an iterative approach to the design of symbols where symbols must be tested for comprehensibility at each cycle in the design process.

ISO/CD 7239: 1984 - Principles for the development and application of public information symbols.

ISO 9241 – 3: 1992 – Ergonomic requirements for office work with visual display terminals (VDT). Part 3: Visual display requirements.

C. The contents of the ISO procedures for the development and testing of public information symbols

The International Standard ISO 9186: 1989 (First edition) specifies the procedure to be used in gathering the information needed to develop Public Information symbols (ISO 7001) as well as the method to be used in testing which variant of a symbol is the most appropriate (in terms, for example, of a specific site or attraction) and the method to be used in testing the extent to which a variant of a symbol communicates its intended message.

Prepared by the Technical Committee ISO/TC 145, (Graphical symbols, Subcommittee SC1, Public Information symbols), this edition is under revision. The new edition is expected for publication in 2000. Its main elements are summarized below.

The procedure involves the use of experts to properly oversee and execute the project of testing symbols using various focus groups made up of the general public.

"Owing to cultural and technological differences between countries, it has been decided to standardize only the image content of graphical symbols, not the graphical images themselves. For each of the image contents included in this International Standard, the details are specified on a single sheet. Each single sheet also contains a guide-line example which conforms to the standard image content. The guideline examples are not binding, but their use is to be encouraged... Where there are two designs, one is suitable for large-scale limits reproduction and the other is simplified for small-scale reproduction; the recommended size limits are shown for each. In such cases, the adaptation for reproduction in very small size may omit some elements of the standard image content."[6]

There are five stages in the procedure for the development and testing of symbols with their image content7:

1. Collection of the information needed concerning the request for a standard symbol.
2. Collection of a set of existing and proposed variants.
3. Selection of the most appropriate variants.
4. Testing of the most appropriate variants.
5. Definition of the standard image content and/or standardization of the most appropriate symbol.

The appropriateness-ranking test is described stage by stage in the International Standard ISO 9186: 1989 as in the following brief:

1. Preparation of test material
   • Information card: Prepare an information card for each referent mentioning the name of the referent, its function, its field(s) of application and excluded functions (if any).
   • Test cards: Make a set of test cards (size A7), each showing one of the symbol variants. On the back of each card, write a code number identifying the referent and the variant.

2. Respondents
   • Conduct the test in at least two countries having different cultural backgrounds (for example, one European country and one Asian country).
   • The number of respondents shall never be less than 50. The validity of the test results will be increased if the sample resembles the eventual user population.

3. Respondents' task
   • Read carefully the information cards.
   • Where there are 10 or fewer variants, the respondent is instructed to rank them from the most appropriate to the least appropriate.
   • Where there are 10 or fewer variants, the respondent is instructed to sort them into three different classes: "very appropriate", "less appropriate" and "least appropriate".

The results of the appropriateness ranking test are tabulated by the

following methodology:
- Sum the values for frequency
- Calculate the median rank value for each variant
- Presentation of the results
- Prepare separate forms for each referent for each country, which participated in the test.

The result forms include such data as:
- the name of the referent
- the function of the referent
- the field(s) of application
- the country in which the test was conducted
- the number of respondents
- copies of the symbol variants tested
- identification codes of the variants
- the source of each variant
- the median rank for each variant

Selection of variants for the comprehension test[8]:

1. Three variants are usually sufficient for the comprehension test.
2. The comprehension test must be conducted in at least four countries.
3. The sample of respondents for one symbol set should comprise at least 100 respondents in each country, with an approximately equal number of respondents from each age group.

Analysis of the results of the comprehension test:

The responses are listed for every referent; the list may be used to resolve any anomalies in the results from different countries. The ISO procedure recommends that 3 judges be appointed to assign each response on the list to one of the seven standard categories from

Correct understanding of the symbol:

- *is certain to the meaning which is stated,*
- *is the opposite of that intended*
- *or the response is wrong[9].*

For the combination of results from different countries, a table is constructed for each referent showing the combined data from all countries, which participated in the comprehension test.

D. Tests using computer screen presentation

The novelty of the draft 2nd edition of the International Standard ISO/DIS 9186: 2 is the introduction of tests using computer screen presentation to be carried out in approved testing centres[10].

For the comprehensibility judgement test, an important step is the preparation of test material:

"To ensure that all displays are of the same standard, they should be prepared at one programming site and the programs and files that made available to the test administrators in each participating country in the format they need. "... During the test a respondent should have a printed version of the information display for the referent. For each respondent, the variant symbols should be positioned in a different random order round the circle on the screen."

For the comprehension test, *"a test-display should show one of the symbols positioned in the centre of the display. The size of the symbol should be at least 40 x 40 mm. Below the symbol should be a rectangular box with a long side of at least 80% of the maximum line length. The box is intended for the respondents' response and should provide space for four lines of text. "In the comprehension test, it is important to inform the respondents of the general context in which they would expect to see the symbol; for example, "at an airport", "on the wall of a public building". This information should be shown on the computer screen above the symbol."*

The new International Standard ISO/DIS 9186: 2 presents also Annex A (normative) for the collection of information. The application form or request form contains the details of the request for the standardization of a symbol or the image content of a symbol. Annex B (normative) on the Comprehensibility judgement test shows a frequency matrix for analyzing the results of the comprehensibility judgement test and the form for presenting the results of the comprehensibility judgement test. Annex C (normative) shows the details of an example of test material for a comprehension test and the Table for presenting the comprehension test as well as the Table for showing the combined data from participating countries for the comprehension test.

[1] see Annex 4: Numerical Index and Survey of the Public Information Symbols adopted in ISO 7001.

[2] The secretariat is hosted by the British Standards Institution (BSI) since December 1996.

[3] Since the start of the Technical Committee (ISO/TC 145), only 57 symbols were developed and adopted, in particular due to the complexity and expense of testing procedures using ISO 9186 Standard. The last edition (second edition) of the ISO 7001 Standard with Amendment 1 was published on 1 February 1990. This edition cancels and replaces the first edition (ISO 7001: 1980) together with ISO 7001: 1980/Addendum 1: 1985, of which it constitutes a minor revision. Source: ISO/TC 145, Resolution 97-2, London. In 1998, the working group of the Technical Committee (ISO/TC 145) on "Graphical symbols" was requested to make proposals for assessment and quick, efficient tests in order to speed up the standardization of public information symbols, especially by using modern electronic means.

[4] On 2-4 November 1998, the Technical Committee ISO/TC 145, SC/1 on Public Information symbols, held a meeting with WTO in Madrid (Spain) and considered the possibility of standardizing new symbols in addition to the already standardized 57 symbols (relating mainly to tourism attractions, tourism sites and tourist equipment).

[5] At the level of the European Committee for Standardization (CEN), in 1999, a proposal was under study (i.e subject to change) which may be, when adopted, the reference for terminology on "Tourism Services – Hotels and other types of tourism accommodation" (Proposal of CEN/TC 329/WG 1) and for terminology on "Tourism Services / Travel Agencies and Tour Operators" (CEN/TC 329/WG 2).

[6] IISO 9186: 1989.

[7] The image content includes the elements of the symbol to test and their relative disposition.

[8] The **comprehension test** is the procedure for eliciting a response from the public which enables measurement of the degree of comprehension of the proposed symbols. This term is different from the **comprehensibility judgement test** which is the procedure for eliciting judgements of the comprehensibility of the proposed symbols.

[9] For the determination of the most comprehensible variant:, a variant giving a score of over 66% (by adding the scores for categories 1 and 2 above) may be used to define the standard image content. Where two variants have the same comprehension score, the most comprehensible variant can be identified by taking the one having the lowest percentage in category 5 ("The response is wrong").

[10] Annex D of the Draft International Standard ISO /DIS 9186: 1999.

CHAPTER III

SELECTED SIGNS AND SYMBOLS, STANDARDIZED, RECOMMENDED AND USED FOR PUBLIC AND VISITOR INFORMATION

1. THE SELECTED CATEGORIES OF REFERENTS

This chapter reviews various signs and symbols (referents) of interest to tourism and their use. They have been selected by the WTO Secretariat on the basis of the material received from member States and other organizations, both national and international. The purpose of the selection is to indicate the possibility of international harmonization of the referents.

As a rule, in the list that follows one example has been taken for each referent, which certainly does not illustrate all the variants of existing signs and symbols. In indicating specific referents, preference was given to those which have already been standardized (ISO), recommended (IUOTO/WTO, IMO, ICAO, UIC), commonly used by a group of countries or uniquely provided by single respondents. However, the quotation of specific referents does not express the preference of the guide drafters, the WTO Secretariat or the Organization. Further, the list of referents does not pretend to be exhaustive as, for example, they may exist graphical symbols for attractions, activities and facilities which may be found only in specific tourism destinations and such have not been included.

The selected referents have been classified into seven main categories:

1. General public and visitor information
2. Tourist equipment and facilities
3. Public and visitor transportation

4. Tourist attractions
5. Sports and outdoor recreation
6. Tourism signs and symbols appearing as typical icons found in Internet portals (open channels) and Web sites

Each referent or variant given in pictogram form in black and white is denoted according to the model below[1]:

- **use** (or symbol function)
- **image content**
- **application**
- **origin of example** (country or organization)
- **comments** (if necessary)

Two hundred and ninety-one referents are represented in this chapter.

---

[1] This description is elaborated by the WTO Secretariat or quoted from ISO (the fifty-seven Public Information symbols adopted in ISO 7001).

General public and visitor information

A. LIST OF REFERENTS

1. Tourist information symbol
2. Way in /Entrance
3. Way out/Exit
4. Emergency exit
5. Directional arrows
6. Stairs
7. Elevator/Lift
8. Escalator
9. No entry/No trespassing
10. Toilets (General)
11. Toilets (Men)
12. Toilets (Women)
13. Fire extinguisher
14. Fire alarm
15. Fire hose
16. Fire phone
17. Telephone
18. Fax facilities/Internet facilities
19. Postal facilities
20. Telegram/Cables/Telex
21. Bank or currency exchange
22. Drinking water (on tap)
23. First aid
24. Pharmacy or drugstore
25. Hospital
26. Garage/Auto mechanics
27. Gasoline station
28. Police/Tourist police
29. Passports / Immigration
30. Customs
31. Lost property/Lost and found
32. Smoking allowed
33. Smoking not allowed
34. Dogs/Pets in leash
35. No dogs allowed
36. Silence
37. School/Kindergarten
38. Pedestrian zone or street
39. Picnic area/Fire place/Outdoor recreation area
40. No fire place
41. Rest area
42. Play area/Playground
43. SOS alarm/Emergency alarm
44. SOS phone
45. Danger/Warning
46. Dangerous water conditions
47. Security camera /Security watching
48. VIP
49. Men's locker
50. Women's locker
51. Sheltered parking
52. No parking
53. Guided tours
54. Litter/Rubbish receptacle
55. No litter
56. International symbol of access for the disabled (persons with disabilities)
57. Accessible to a wheelchair user with assistance
58. Access to someone with limited mobility but able to walk a few paces and up to a maximum of three steps
59. Access for persons with walking aids
60. Facilities for visually impaired persons

61. Facilities for persons with hearing impairments
62. Guide dogs welcome
63. Information in Braille
64. Facilities for older persons
65. Facilities for pregnant women
66. Facilities for women with baby
67. Facilities for persons with cardiac disabilities
68. Facilities for persons with mental disabilities

B. DESCRIPTION OF REFERENTS

Tourist information symbol

Use: To indicate and identify the location of an tourist information point or place

Image content: *i or i?* or i or i?, a blue letter in a white square with blue background

Application: Buildings, public places, maps, guidebooks, orientation diagrams

Origin of example: WTO

Way in/Entrance

Use: To indicate and identify the location of an entry or preferred way to enter

Image content: Diagram enclosure with top view of two swing doors in one side of enclosure. Doors are partially opened inwards with arrow head in opening.

Application: Buildings, public places, maps, guidebooks, orientation diagrams, vehicles

Origin of example: ISO 7001

Way out /Exit

Use: To indicate and identify the location of an entry or preferred way to go out

Image content: Diagram enclosure with top view of two swing doors in one side of enclosure. Doors are partially opened outwards with arrowhead in opening.

Application: Buildings, public places, maps, guidebooks, orientation diagrams, vehicles

Origin of example: ISO 7001

Emergency exit

Use: To indicate and identify the location of an emergency exit or preferred way to go out in case of emergency or fire

Image content: Silhouetted human figure running out of door

Application: Buildings, public places, maps, guidebooks, orientation diagrams, vehicles

Origin of example: China

Directional arrows

Use: To indicate direction
Image content: Arrow with Belgian head and angle at apex of between 84º and 86º
Application: Buildings, public places and vehicles
Origin of example: ISO 7001

Stairs

Use: To signify access facilities via a fixed staircase. Shall not be used to indicate or identify an escalator
Image content:
   (a) where no direction is required: staircase with two human figures, one walking up, one walking down
   (b) for staircases restricted to "down" traffic: staircase with one human figure walking down
   (c) for staircases restricted to "up" traffic: staircase with one human figure walking up
Application: Buildings, public places, vehicles
Origin of example: ISO 7001

Elevator/Lift

Use: To indicate and identify the location of a public elevator (lift)
Image content: Lift (elevator) cage in lift (elevator) shaft showing several pushbuttons on lift (elevator) cage. Figure in cage. "Up" arrow above the cage. "Down" arrow below the cage.
Application: Buildings, public places, orientation diagrams
Origin of example: ISO 7001

No entry/No trespassing

Use: To prohibit the entrance in a street, road, path, trail or a place, corridor, room, etc.
Image content: Red circle with white strip in the middle
Application: Buildings, public places, streets and roads, orientation diagrams, vehicles, rooms, corridors, etc.
Origin of example: Convention on road signs and signals, ICAO/IMO

Toilets (General)

Use: To indicate the entrance of a public toilet for men and women

Image content: Front perspective of man and woman figures separated by a wall-line

Application: Buildings, public places, orientation diagrams, and vehicles

Origin of example: Portugal

Toilets (Men)

Use: To indicate the entrance of a public toilet for men

Image content: Front perspective of man figure

Application: Buildings, public places, orientation diagrams, and vehicles

Origin of example: ICAO/IMO

Toilets (Women)

Use: To indicate the entrance of a public toilet for women

Image content: Front perspective of woman figure

Application: Buildings, public places, orientation diagrams, and vehicles

Origin of example: ICAO/IMO

Fire extinguisher

Use: To indicate the location of a fire extinguisher and/or to identify a fire extinguisher

Image content: Cylinder fire extinguisher with tap adjacent to flames

Application: Buildings, public transportation facilities, bridges, tunnels, recreational areas

Origin of example: ISO 7001

Fire alarm

Use: To indicate the location of a fire alarm and/or to identify a fire alarm

Image content: Hand pushing button adjacent to flames

Application: Buildings, public transportation facilities, bridges, tunnels, recreational areas

Origin of example: China

Fire hose

Use: To indicate the location of a fire hose and/or to identify a fire hose

Image content: A square diagram representing a rolled up fire hose

Application: Buildings, public transportation facilities, bridges, tunnels, recreational areas

Origin of example: AH&MA

Fire phone

Use: To indicate the location of a fire alarm phone and/or to identify a fire alarm phone

Image content: A square diagram with telephone receiver in profile

Application: Buildings, public transportation facilities, bridges, tunnels, recreational areas

Origin of example: AH&MA

Telephone

Use: To signify communication facilities by telephone

Image content: Telephone receiver in profile

Application: Buildings, public places, orientation maps, vehicles

Origin of example: ISO 7001

Fax facilities/Internet facilities

Use: To signify communication facilities by fax or Internet

Image content:

1. Radar antenna and telephone receiver in profile
2. Telephone receiver in profile with a electrical flash (example)
3. World Globe with blue arrows (International)

Application: Buildings, public places, orientation maps

Origin of example: Portugal, Internet icon

Postal facilities

Use: To signify or to indicate the place where postal facilities can be found

Image content: Diagram of a stamped envelope with two lines representing an address

Application: Buildings, public places, orientation maps

Origin of example: ICAO/IMO

Telegram/Cables/Telex

Use: To signify or to indicate the place where telegram/cables/telex facilities can be found

Image content: Diagram of a stamped envelope with electrical flash

Application: Buildings, public places, orientation maps

Origin of example: ICAO/IMO

Bank or currency exchange

Use: To signify or to indicate the location of a bank or an office where foreign money may be exchanged

Image content: Banknote with numbers as currency mark and three randomly arranged coins each with a different number (i.e. 25, 10 and 5)

Application: Buildings, public places, orientation maps

Origin of example: ICAO/IMO

Drinking water (on tap)

Use: To signify drinking (tap) water

Image content: Tap above glass containing water indicated by wavy lines

Application: Buildings, public places, orientation diagrams, vehicles

Origin of example: ISO 7001

First aid

Use: To indicate the place where a first aid service (or even kit) or a doctor is available

Image content: Human hand with banded finger adjacent to a cross, crescent or another appropriate emblem in green or red colour

Application: Buildings, public places, guidebooks, orientation diagrams, vehicles

Origin of example: China

Pharmacy or drugstore

Use: To indicate the place where a pharmacy or a drugstore (where medicines can be sold) is located

Image content: Aesculapus's caduceus showing a snake around a rod in side view in a plain double-cross

Application: Buildings, public places, guidebooks, orientation diagrams

Origin of example: China (Macao)

Hospital

Use: To indicate where permanent medical service is available and/or to identify the building itself and the connecting area

Image content: Bed with cross or crescent above in outline (or other emblem used in the country)

Application: Buildings, public places, maps, guidebooks, orientation diagrams

Origin of example: ISO 7001

Garage/Auto mechanics

Use: To signify the availability of auto repairs and motor fuel

Image content: Outline of an adjustable spanner

Application: Buildings, public places, maps, guidebooks, orientation diagrams

Origin of example: Portugal

Gasoline station

Use: To signify the availability of motor fuel

Image content: Gasoline pumps with hose to show different types of fuel (unleaded gas)

Application: Buildings, public places, maps, guidebooks, orientation diagrams

Origin of example: ISO 7001

Police/Tourist police

Use: To indicate and identify the location of a police station or a place where a policeman or a tourist policeman can be found

Image content: Policeman in uniform in front view

Application: Buildings, public places, maps, guidebooks, orientation diagrams

Origin of example: Argentina

Comment: In some countries, only the logotype of the tourist police is used.

Passports/Immigration

Use: To indicate and identify the location of a passport or immigration booth or office

Image content: Human figure of officer handling a passport

Application: Public places, orientation diagrams

Origin of example: ICAO/IMO

Customs

Use: To indicate and identify the location of customs

Image content: Human figure of officer looking to open luggage

Application: Public places, orientation diagrams

Origin of example: Argentina

Lost property/Lost and found

Use: To indicate and identify the location where lost property may be registered or property that has been found may be claimed

Image content: Glove, umbrella with label displaying a question mark and briefcase

Application: Buildings and public places, orientation diagrams

Origin of example: ISO 7001

Smoking allowed

Use: To signify where smoking is allowed
Image content: Cigarette with smoke view
Application: Buildings, public places, services, vehicles
Origin of example: ISO 7001

Smoking not allowed

Use: To signify where smoking is not allowed
Image content: Cigarette with smoke view with a diagonal slash bar
Application: Buildings, public places, services, vehicles
Origin of example: IMO/ICAO

Dogs/Pets on leash

Use: To indicate the possibility to walk or jog with pets, dogs on leash/led
Image content: Human figure in side view with dog figure on a leash in side view
Application: Buildings, public places, guidebooks, orientation diagrams
Origin of example: AH&MA

No dogs allowed

Use: To indicate that no dogs are allowed
Image content: Dog figure in side view with a prohibition slash
Application: Buildings, public places, guidebooks, orientation diagrams, vehicles
Origin of example: Austria

Silence

Use: To signify the need of silence in a shrine or a specific place
Image content: A hand with a finger pointing lips
Application: Buildings, shrines, halls, special sites or places
Origin of example: China

School/Kindergarten

Use: To indicate the existence of a school and to prevent drivers of the presence of children

Image content: The figure of two kids running (a boy figure and a girl figure in side view) with school satchels

Application: Street and public places

Origin of example: Portugal

Pedestrian zone or street

Use: To indicate the existence of a zone or a street where private cars are forbidden and where visitors have to walk

Image content: The figure of adults and kids walking in front view

Application: Street and public places, orientation diagrams, maps

Origin of example: Portugal, China (Macao)

Picnic area/Fire place/Outdoor recreation area

1

Use: To indicate a outdoor recreation place or a place in a road or motorway rest area where picnicking is possible with or not fire place(s)

Image content: Outdoor table in side view with a fire place if it exists or a table with a seated human figure

Application: Roads and motorways, outdoor recreation areas, maps, guidebooks, orientation diagrams

Origin of example: Argentina (1); Austria (2)

2

Fire place

Use: To indicate a place where fire is prohibited for picnicking or other activities

Image content: Firewood circle with flames

Application: Roads and motorways, outdoor recreation areas, maps, guidebooks, orientation diagrams

Origin of example: Austria

Rest area

Use: To indicate an outdoor recreation place or a place on a side of a road or motorway where rest is possible with or without picnicking facilities
Image content: A deck chair
Application: Roads and motorways, outdoor recreation areas, maps, guidebooks, orientation diagrams
Origin of example: Portugal

Play area/Playground

Use: To indicate an outdoor recreation ground or a place on a side of a road or motorway with outdoor playing facilities is possible for adults or kids
Image content: Swing in side view with kids or human figures
Application: Roads and motorways, outdoor recreation areas, maps, guidebooks, orientation diagrams
Origin of example: Austria

SOS alarm/Emergency alarm

Use: To indicate the location of and/or to identify an alarm signal
Image content: SOS in Latin block capital letters
Application: Buildings, public transportation facilities, bridges, tunnels, recreational areas
Origin of example: China

SOS phone

Use: To indicate the location of and/or to identify an alarm phone
Image content: A phone handle adjacent to SOS in Latin block capital letters
Application: Buildings, public transportation facilities, bridges, tunnels, recreational areas
Origin of example: China

Danger/Warning

Use: To warn or indicate dangerous conditions
Image content: Exclamation mark
Application: Roads and motorways, coasts, outdoor recreation areas
Origin of example: New Zealand

Dangerous water conditions

Use: To warn of dangerous water conditions
Image content: Exclamation mark above two wavy lines
Application: Roads and motorways, coasts, outdoor recreation areas
Origin of example: New Zealand

Security camera/Security watching

Use: To indicate and identify the location of a security camera or a zone with security watching
Image content: Diagram enclosure with top view of two swing doors in one side of enclosure. Doors are partially opened outwards with arrowhead in opening.
Application: Buildings, public places, and public transportation vehicles
Origin of example: Portugal

VIP

Use: To indicate a room, a zone or a place only allowed to VIP and authorized personnel
Image content: VIP in Latin block capital letters
Application: Public transportation terminals, buildings, hotels, convention centers or special places
Origin of example: China

Men's locker

Use: To indicate and identify the location of men's locker
Image content: Male figure and coat-hanger
Application: Buildings, public places, orientation diagrams, vehicles
Origin of example: China

Women's locker

Use: To indicate and identify the location of women's locker
Image content: Female figure and coat-hanger
Application: Buildings, public places, orientation diagrams, vehicles
Origin of example: China

Sheltered parking

Use: To indicate and identify the location of a sheltered area where vehicles may be parked
Image content: Sanserif capital letter "P" under symbol representing sheltering facility
Application: Buildings, public places, shopping centers, maps, guidebooks, orientation diagrams
Origin of example: Portugal

No parking

Use: To indicate and identify the location of a sheltered area where vehicles may be parked
Image content: Sanserif capital letter "P" with prohibition slash
Application: Buildings, public places, shopping centers, maps, guidebooks, orientation diagrams
Origin of example: Austria

Guided tours

Use: To indicate the possibility and the location of guided tours in a city, tourist area, park, outdoor recreation area
Image content: Human figure in side view along to a bus in front view with the word "TOUR" in capital letters
Application: Orientation diagrams, public places
Origin of example: Portugal

Litter/Rubbish receptacle

Use: To indicate a receptacle where rubbish may be thrown away
Image content: Standing figure adjacent to sectional elevation of a rubbish receptacle. Four representative articles of rubbish falling down into the receptacle
Application: Buildings, public places, maps, guidebooks, orientation diagrams, vehicles
Origin of example: variant of ISO 7001

No litter

Use: To indicate the prohibition of littering rubbish
Image content: Hand with slashed litter
Application: Buildings, public places, maps, guidebooks, orientation diagrams, vehicles
Origin of example: ISO 7001

International symbol
of access for the disabled

Use: To indicate the possibility for persons with limited mobility to have access to a place, hall, room, bathroom or toilets, etc.
Image content: Human figure seated on a wheelchair in side view
Application: Buildings, public places, maps, guidebooks, orientation diagrams, vehicles
Origin of example: Rehabilitation International (RI)

Accessible to a wheelchair
user with assistance

Use: To indicate the possibility for persons with limited mobility to have access to a place, hall, room, bathroom or toilets, etc. with the assistance of another person

Image content: Standing human figure behind a human figure seated on a wheelchair in side view

Application: Buildings, public places, public transportation modes, maps, guidebooks, orientation diagrams

Origin of example: variant of the symbol adopted in 1969 by Rehabilitation International (RI)

Access to someone with limited
mobility but able to walk a few paces
and up to a maximum of three steps

Use: To indicate the possibility for persons with limited mobility but able to walk a few paces and up to a maximum of three steps to have access to a place, hall, room, bathroom or toilets, etc.

Image content: Standing human figure with a walking stick or a tripod stick

Application: Buildings, public places, public transportation modes, guidebooks, orientation diagrams

Origin of example: Proposal of the European Union Tourism For All Accessible Accommodation Standard

Access for persons with walking aids

Use: To indicate the possibility for persons with limited mobility but able to walk with walking aids to have access to a place, hall, room, bathroom or toilets, etc.

Image content: Standing human figure with one or two crutches

Application: Buildings, public places, public transportation modes, guidebooks, orientation diagrams

Origin of example: Proposal of the European Union Tourism For All Accessible Accommodation Standard

Facilities for visually impaired people

Use: To indicate facilities for visually impaired people (blind or partially sighted people), with or without tapping cane, to have access to a place, hall, room, bathroom or toilets, etc.

Image content: Sectional eye drawing with slash and fractured left side

Application: Buildings, public places, public transportation modes, guidebooks, orientation diagrams

Origin of example: Proposal of the European Union Tourism For All Accessible Accommodation Standard

Facilities for persons with hearing impairments

Use: To indicate facilities for persons with hearing impairments (deaf, deaf without speech or hard of hearing) to have access to a place, hall, room, bathroom or toilets, etc.

Image content: Ear with large plain diagonal slash

Application: Buildings, public places, public transportation modes, guidebooks, orientation diagrams

Origin of example: Proposal of the European Union Tourism For All Accessible Accommodation Standard

Origin of example: ISO 7001

Comment: International symbol used to show induction loop is available. Also used to show that staff have skills in helping deaf people or that there are other facilities for deaf people

Guide dogs welcome

Use: To indicate the possibility for persons with disabilities assisted by a guide dog to have access to a place or establishment

Image content: Standing human figure helped by a guide dog on a leash

Application: Buildings, public places, public transportation modes, guidebooks, orientation diagrams

Origin of example: Proposal of the European Union Tourism For All Accessible Accommodation Standard

Information in Braille

Use: To indicate the existence of information in Braille for visually impaired people (blind or partially sighted people)
Image content: Diagram enclosure with Braille alphabet
Application: Buildings, public places, public transportation modes, guidebooks, orientation diagrams
Origin of example: Proposal of the European Union Tourism For All Accessible Accommodation Standard

Facilities for older persons

Use: To indicate the existence of facilities for old people
Image content: Human figure bent with cane
Application: Buildings, public places, public transportation modes, orientation diagrams
Origin of example: ALPE Proposal

Facilities for pregnant women

Use: To indicate the existence of facilities for pregnant women
Image content: Human figure of pregnant woman in side view
Application: Buildings, public places, public transportation modes, orientation diagrams
Origin of example: ALPE Proposal

Facilities for women with baby

Use: To indicate the existence of facilities for women with baby
Image content: Human figure of woman with baby in front view
Application: Buildings, public places, public transportation modes, orientation diagrams
Origin of example: ALPE Proposal

Facilities for persons with cardiac disabilities

Use: To indicate the existence of facilities for persons with cardiac disabilities
Image content: Plain human figure with white circle on heart in front view
Application: Buildings, public places, public transportation modes, orientation diagrams
Origin of example: ALPE Proposal

Facilities for persons with mental disabilities

Use: To indicate the existence of facilities for persons with mental disabilities

Image content: Plain human figure with white circle head in front view

Application: Buildings, public places, public transportation modes, orientation diagrams

Origin of example: ALPE Proposal

Tourist equipment and facilities

A. LIST OF REFERENTS

1. Accommodation
2. Restaurant
3. Hotel
4. Motel
5. Tourist apartment
6. Campsite/Camping area
7. Camping not allowed
8. Caravan/Mobile home park
9. Power point (electric energy point)
10. Youth hostel
11. Inn/Country hotel
12. Mountain refuge or other refuge
13. Casino
14. Mahjong
15. Cards and chess
16. Conference facilities
17. Conference /Meeting room
18. Banquet room
19. Business centre
20. Night club/Dance hall
21. Karaoke bar
22. Bar
23. National thematic restaurant
24. Snack bar
25. Coffee/Tea room
26. Swimming place
27. Sauna
28. Massage
29. Check-in/out or reception
30. Breakfast only
31. Facilities for children
32. Hairdresser/Beauty salon/ Barber
33. Dry cleaning
34. Laundry service
35. Room service

B. DESCRIPTION OF REFERENTS

Accommodation

Use: To indicate and identify where temporary accommodation is available or may be booked
Image content: Sleeping figure in bed
Application: Buildings, services, public places, maps, guidebooks, orientation diagrams
Origin of example: ISO 7001

Restaurant

Use: To indicate an eating place where hot and cold meals are available and which is licensed to serve wine and spirits
Image content: Diagonally crossed knife and fork
Application: Buildings, services, public places, maps, guidebooks, orientation diagrams
Origin of example: ISO 7001

Hotel

Use: To indicate and identify where hotel accommodation is available or may be booked
Image content: Sleeping figure in bed under a shelter house
Application: Buildings, services, public places, maps, guidebooks, orientation diagrams
Origin of example: Argentina

Motel

Use: To indicate and identify where motel accommodation is available or may be booked
Image content: Bed under one side of a shelter, a private car on the other side
Application: Buildings, services, public places, maps, guidebooks, orientation diagrams
Origin of example: Argentina

Tourist apartment

Use: To indicate and identify where tourist apartment is available or may be booked

Image content: Sleeping figure in bed under a shelter with a large A or large A over white stripe

Application: Buildings, services, public places, maps, guidebooks, orientation diagrams

Origin of example: Portugal

Camp site/Camping area

Use: To indicate the location of a camp site or a camping area

Image content: Bell tent with door in front view

Application: Outdoor recreation areas, maps, guidebooks, orientation diagrams

Origin of example: Austria

Camping not allowed

Use: To prohibit camping

Image content: Tent with door in front view with a prohibition slash

Application: Outdoor recreation areas, orientation diagrams

Origin of example: Austria

Caravan/mobile home park

Use: To indicate the location of a caravan site or a mobile home park

Image content: Caravan in side view

Application: Outdoor recreation areas, maps, guidebooks, orientation diagrams

Origin of example: China (Macao)

Power point
(electric energy point)

Use: To indicate the availability of power points in a camp site or outdoor recreation area

Image content: Plug (in front view) and socket (side view) connectors

Application: Outdoor recreation areas, maps, guidebooks, orientation diagrams

Origin of example: Portugal

Youth hostel

Use: To indicate the location of a youth hostel
Image content: Linear drawing of a house with a tree
Application: Outdoor recreation areas, maps, guidebooks, orientation diagrams
Origin of example: International Federation of Youth Hostels

Inn/Country hotel

Use: To indicate the location of a inn or a country hotel
Image content: Silhouetted drawing of a house
Application: Outdoor recreation areas, maps, guidebooks, orientation diagrams
Origin of example: China (Macao)

Mountain refuge or other refuge

Use: To indicate the location of a mountain refuge or refuge
Image content: Linear drawing of a shelter with a human figure in front of a chimney
Application: Outdoor recreation areas, maps, guidebooks, orientation diagrams
Origin of example: Argentina

Casino

Use: To indicate and identify the location of a casino
Image content: Linear drawing of two playing cards (aces)
Application: Buildings, services, public places, maps, guidebooks, orientation diagrams
Origin of example: Argentina

Mahjong

Use: To indicate and identify the location of a mahjong room
Image content: Linear drawing of two dice
Application: Buildings, services, orientation diagrams
Origin of example: China

Cards and chess

Use: To indicate and identify the location of a room where it is possible to play chess and cards
Image content: Card and chess symbols
Application: Buildings, services, orientation diagrams
Origin of example: China

Conference facilities

Use: To indicate and identify the location of a conference center or meeting facilities

Image content: A meeting hall with human figures seated

Application: Buildings, services, orientation diagrams, maps, guidebooks

Origin of example: Portugal

Conference/Meeting room

Use: To indicate and identify the location and the availability of a conference or meeting room

Image content: Four human torso figures around a table

Application: Buildings, services, orientation diagrams

Origin of example: China

Banquet room

Use: To indicate and identify the location of a banquet room

Image content: Three human torso figures around a table with fork and spoon

Application: Buildings, orientation diagrams

Origin of example: Portugal

Business center

Use: To indicate and identify the location of a business center

Image content: Linear drawing of a type writer and a written page

Application: Public places, buildings, orientation diagrams

Origin of example: China

Nightclub/Dance hall

Use: To indicate and identify the location of night club or dance hall

Image content: Female and male human figures dancing

Application: Buildings, services, public places, orientation diagrams, maps, guidebooks

Origin of example: China

Karaoke Bar

Use: To indicate and identify the location of karaoke bar or a place where karaoke can be found
Image content: Hand holding a microphone and treble clef
Application: Buildings, services, public places, orientation diagrams, maps, guidebooks
Origin of example: China

Bar

Use: To indicate and identify the location of bar (licensed or not)
Image content: Linear drawing of a coctail glass
Application: Buildings, services, public places, orientation diagrams, maps, guidebooks
Origin of example: ICAO/IMO

National thematic restaurant

Use: To indicate and identify the location of eating place where national thematic hot and cold meals are available, licensed or not
Image content: Depending on the national or local culture in China, a soup bowl and two sticks
Application: Buildings, services, public places, orientation diagrams, maps, guidebooks
Origin of example: China

Snack bar

Use: To indicate and identify the location of eating place where hot and cold meals are quickly served, licensed or not
Image content: A soft drink glass and a hamburger
Application: Buildings, services, public places, orientation diagrams, maps
Origin of example: China

Coffee/Tea room

Use: To indicate and identify the location of coffee shop or a tea room where cold and hot drinks are available

Image content: Linear drawing of a coffee or a tea cup with three lines up symbolizing heat

Application: Buildings, services, public places, orientation diagrams, maps

Origin of example: China

Swimming place

Use: To indicate and identify the location of a public swimming place or pool or a private swimming place in a accommodation establishment

Image content: Depending on the national or local culture, in general a human figure on a diving board above three waves

Application: Buildings, services, public places, orientation diagrams, maps

Origin of example: China (Macao)

Sauna

Use: To indicate and identify the location of a sauna room or where a sauna is available in an accommodation establishment

Image content: Human figure seated in front of a heat source

Application: Buildings, services, orientation diagrams

Origin of example: China

Massage

Use: To indicate and identify the location of a message place or where massage is available in a accommodation establishment

Image content: Human figure lying down on a massage table with another human torso giving massage

Application: Buildings, services, orientation diagrams

Origin of example: China

Check-in/out or reception

Use: To indicate and identify the location of a reception or a check-in counter in an accommodation establishment
Image content: Human torso behind a bar and another human figure waiting with luggage on the floor
Application: Buildings, services, orientation diagrams
Origin of example: China

Breakfast only

Use: To indicate that only breakfast are served in an accommodation establishment
Image content: Coffee cup and egg cup
Application: Buildings, services, orientation diagrams
Origin of example: Portugal

Facilities for children

Use: To indicate and identify facilities for children/infants
Image content: Linear drawing of Child's push chair
Application: Buildings, services, orientation diagrams
Origin of example: Austria

Hairdresser/Beauty salon/Barber

Use: To indicate and identify hairdresser, beauty or barber facilities in a public place or an accommodation establishment
Image content: Linear drawing of a pair of scissors and a comb
Application: Buildings, services, orientation diagrams
Origin of example: China

Dry cleaning

Use: To indicate and identify dry cleaning facilities in a public place or an accommodation establishment
Image content: Linear drawing of a shirt or over-garment being dried
Application: Buildings, services, orientation diagrams
Origin of example: China

Laundry service

Use: To indicate and identify laundry facilities in a public place or an accommodation establishment

Image content: Linear drawing of a shirt or over-garment being laundered

Application: Buildings, services, orientation diagrams

Origin of example: China

Room service

Use: To indicate that room service is available in an accommodation establishment

Image content: Human figure holding a food and beverage tray in side view in a corridor

Application: Buildings, services, orientation diagrams

Origin of example: China

Public and visitor transportation

A. LIST OF REFERENTS

(a) ICAO/IMO recommended symbols

The ISO 7001 standardized symbols, the ICAO/IMO recommended symbols which coincide with ISO/7001 are not included in this section:

1. Baggage claim area
2. Baggage cart/trolley
3. Baggage lockers
4. Train
5. Car hire/Car reservations
6. Shopping area
7. Variant 1: Flowers (China)
8. Nursery/Baby care
9. Hotel reservations
10. Carry no weapons on board
11. Arrivals (airports)
12. Arrivals (marine)
13. Departures (airports)
14. Departures (marine)
15. Connecting flights
16. Foot passengers
17. Cars
18. Lorries

(b) ISO 7001 standardized symbols (coinciding with the ICAO/IMO recommended symbols)

19. Helicopter
20. Tram streetcar
21. Bus

22. Taxi
23. Waiting room
24. Aircraft
25. Boat
26. Left luggage

(c) Other ISO 7001 standards linked with public and visitor transportation

27. Cable car, large capacity
28. Cable car, small capacity
29. Cable railway / ratchet railway
30. Chair lift
31. Close overhead safety bar
32. Open overhead safety bar
33. Close safety bar
34. Open safety bar
35. Line up two by two
36. Line up three by three
37. Raise ski tips
38. Ski lift
39. Bath
40. Shower
41. Tickets
42. Double Chairlift
43. Triple Chairlift
44. Quadruple Chairlift
45. Line up four by four
46. Foot passengers have to get off
47. Skiers have to get off
48. Steep-slope ski lift

(d) Other transportation symbols (designed by international bodies and at national level)

49. Old forms of transportation
50. High speed train
51. Underground station/Metro
52. Air strip
53. Meeting point
54. Prayer place
55. Seaport
56. Cruise boat
57. Anchorage
58. Mooring point
59. Boat launching

B. DESCRIPTION OF REFERENTS

Baggage claim area

Use: To indicate the location in an airport or any transportation system where luggage are distributed
Image content: A piece of luggage arranged on a convoyer belt
Application: Public places, orientation diagrams
Origin of example: ICAO/IMO

Baggage cart/ trolley

Use: To indicate the existence and location of baggage trolleys in an airport hall, seaport hall or any other public transportation system
Image content: Baggage cart in side view with a piece of luggage
Application: Public places, orientation diagrams
Origin of example: ICAO/IMO

Baggage lockers

Use: To indicate the existence and location of baggage lockers in an airport hall, seaport hall or any other public transportation system
Image content: Baggage locker with luggage under a drawn key
Application: Public places, orientation diagrams
Origin of example: ICAO/IMO

Train

Use: To indicate the location of a railway station
Image content: Train in front or side view
Application: Public places, streets and roads, orientation diagrams, guidebooks, maps, timetables
Origin of example: ICAO/IMO

Car hire/Car reservations

Use: To indicate the possibility of car hire, the existence and the location of a car reservation booth

Image content: Linear drawn key above a car in front view

Application: Buildings, public places, streets and roads, orientation diagrams, vehicles, rooms, corridors, etc.

Origin of example: ICAO/IMO

Comment: a "i" may be added to the key symbol

Shopping area

Use: To indicate the existence and location of a shopping center in a public transportation place

Image content: Stylized book and newspaper drawings

Application: Buildings, public places, orientation diagrams

Origin of example: ICAO/IMO

Variant 1: Flowers (China)

Use: To indicate the existence and location of a shopping center in a public transportation place with a flower shop

Image content: Stylized flower drawing

Application: Buildings, public places, orientation diagrams

Origin of example: China

Nursery/Baby care

Use: To indicate the existence and location of a nursery or a baby care room in a public place (mainly airport, seaport, railway or bus terminals)

Image content: Drawing of a feeding bottle

Application: Public places, orientation diagrams, vehicles

Origin of example: ICAO/IMO

Comment: in some countries, the image contents a female figure caring infant

Hotel reservations

Use: To indicate the possibility, the existence and the location of a hotel reservation booth

Image content: Question mark above a bed in side view

Application: Public places, orientation diagrams

Origin of example: ICAO/IMO

Comment: The question mark "?" may be changed by "i" or "i"

Carry no weapons on board

Use: To prohibit the entrance on board of a plane or a ship with weapons
Image content: Red circle with red strip in the middle around knife and handgun
Application: Airports, seaports
Origin of example: ICAO/IMO

Arrivals (airports)

Use: To indicate arrival zone at airport
Image content: Silhouette of boeing landing over airstrip depicted by a stripe below it
Application: Air terminals
Origin of example: ICAO/IMO

Arrivals (marine)

Use: To indicate arrival zone at harbour
Image content: Frontal image of boat and a broken square with wavy line drawings above it depicting the harbour entrance
Application: Marine terminals
Origin of example: ICAO/IMO

Departure (airports)

Use: To indicate the departure zone at airport.
Image content: Silhouetted drawing of boeing taking off from airstrip depicted by a stripe below it
Application: Air terminals
Origin of example: ICAO/IMO

Departure (marine)

Use: To indicate departure zone at harbour.
Image content: Frontal image of boat and a broken square with wavy line drawings above it depicting the harbour exit
Application: Marine terminals
Origin of example: ICAO/IMO

Connecting flights

Use: To show the location of transit and connecting area in an airport

Image content: Two planes linked by a line and human figures walking between

Application: Air terminals

Origin of example: ICAO/IMO

Pedestrians

Use: To indicate the path or way for pedestrians.

Image content: A male and female figure in walking posture above an arrow

Application: Buildings, public places, streets and roads, rooms, corridors, etc.

Origin of example: ICAO/IMO

Cars

Use: To indicate the road or way for cars.

Image content: Frontal image of a car above an arrow

Application: Air and marine terminals and train stations

Origin of example: ICAO/IMO

Lorries

Use: To prohibit the entrance in a street, road, path, trail or a place, corridor, room, etc.

Image content: Drawing of a truck from front left angle

Application: Air and marine terminals and train stations

Origin of example: ICAO/IMO

Helicopter

Use: To signify a transport facility by helicopter

Image content: Helicopter in side view

Application: Buildings, services, public places, maps, guide-books, and timetables

Origin of example: ISO 7001

Tram streetcar

Use: To signify a transport facility by tram (streetcar)
Image content: Electric tram (streetcar) in side view
Application: Buildings, services, public places, maps, guidebooks, and timetables
Origin of example: ISO 7001

Bus

Use: To signify a transport facility by bus
Image content: Bus in side view
Application: Buildings, services, public places, maps, guidebooks, and timetables
Origin of example: ISO 7001

Taxi

Use: To signify a transport facility by taxi
Image content: Front view of taxicab with "TAXI" incorporated into the symbol. For small reproduction the word "TAXI" may be omitted
Application: Buildings, services, public places, maps, guidebooks, timetables, orientation diagrams
Origin of example: ISO 7001

Waiting room

Use: To signify areas where people may wait
Image content: Two persons in side view with a clock overhead
Application: Buildings, services, public places, maps, guidebooks, and timetables
Origin of example: ISO 7001

Boat

Use: To indicate the location of a ferry or water transport services or to identify them
Image content: Side view of appropriate water transport
Application: Buildings, services, public places, maps, guidebooks, orientation diagrams, timetables
Origin of example: ISO 7001

Aircraft

Use: To signify the location of an airport
Image content: Aircraft in plan view
Application: Buildings, services, public places, maps, guidebooks, timetables, orientation diagrams
Origin of example: ISO 7001

Left luggage

Use: To indicate a supervised place for temporary storage of luggage
Image content: Four assorted pieces of luggage arranged on two shelves in orderly fashion
Application: Buildings, services, public places, maps, guidebooks, orientation diagrams, vehicles, rooms, corridors, etc.
Origin of example: ISO 7001

Cable car, large capacity

Use: To indicate and identify cable car transport where passengers travel in suspended closed car of large capacity
Image content: Large rectangular cable car with several windows, suspended from an inclined cable, in side view
Application: Ski and tourist resorts, sign boards, maps, guidebooks, orientation diagrams
.Origin of example: ISO 7001

Cable car, small capacity

Use: To indicate and identify cable car transport where passengers travel in suspended closed car of small capacity
Image content: Small hexagonal cable car with one window suspended from an inclined cable, in side view
Application: Ski and tourist resorts, sign boards, maps, guidebooks, orientation diagrams
Origin of example: ISO 7001

Cable railway/ratchet railway

Use: To indicate transport by cable railway (ratchet railway) where passengers travel in closed cars
Image content: Car of cable railway (ratchet railway)
Application: Ski and tourist resorts, sign boards, maps, guidebooks, orientation diagrams
Origin of example: ISO 7001

Chair lift

Use: To indicate transport where passengers travel singly on suspended chairs

Image content: Human figure seated on a chair with attachment suspended from an inclined cable, in side view

Application: Ski and tourist resorts, sign boards, maps, guidebooks, orientation diagrams

Origin of example: ISO 7001

Close overhead safety bar

Use: To instruct passengers to close the overhead safety bar immediately after boarding

Image content: Human figure seated on a chair in side view, closing an overhead safety bar; an arrow indicates the direction of movement

Application: Chairs lifts with overhead safety bars

Origin of example: ISO 7001

Open overhead safety bar

Use: To indicate the point at which the chair lift passengers approaching the top or lower station have to open the overhead safety bar

Image content: Human figure seated on a chair in side view, closing an overhead safety bar; an arrow indicates the direction of movement

Application: Chairs lifts with overhead safety bars

Origin of example: ISO 7001

Close safety bar

Use: To instruct passengers to close the safety bar (safety chain) immediately after boarding

Image content: Suspended chair with attachment and safety bar in front view; an arrow indicates the movement of closing

Application: Chairs lifts with safety bars (safety chains)

Origin of example: ISO 7001

Open safety bar

Use: To indicate the point at which the chair lift passengers approaching the top or lower station have to open the safety bar (chain)

Image content: Suspended chair with attachment and safety bar in front view; an arrow indicates the movement of opening

Application: Chairs lifts with safety bars (safety chains)

Origin of example: ISO 7001

Line up two by two

Use: To instruct passengers to line up two by two

Image content: Two human figures drawn in solid form standing side by side in front view, behind each of which are similar figures drawn in outline

Application: Double chair lifts, T-bar ski lifts

Origin of example: ISO 7001

Line up three by three

Use: To instruct passengers to line up three by three

Image content: Three human figures drawn in solid form standing side by side in front view, behind each of which are similar figures drawn in outline

Application: Triple chair lifts

Origin of example: ISO 7001

Raise ski tips

Use: To indicate the point at which passengers must raise the tips of the skis

Image content: Human figures drawn in solid form seated on a suspended chair in side view, with an upward arrow adjacent to the ski tips

Application: Chair lifts

Origin of example: ISO 7001

Ski lift

Use: To indicate ski lift transportation intended only for people on skis

Image content: Human figure seated on skis in side view holding a rope that points in the direction of movement

Application: Ski and tourist resorts, sign boards, maps, guidebooks, orientation diagrams

Origin of example: ISO 7001

Bath

Use: To indicate and identify a location where an indoor facility for partial immersion of the human body in water in a near-horizontal position is available. Not for shower or swimming-pool

Image content: Silhouette of human figure in bath in water indicated by a wavy line

Application: Buildings and other locations, floor plans, maps, guidebooks, orientation diagrams

Origin of example: ISO 7001

Shower

Use: To indicate and identify a facility for washing by continuous dispersed flow of water over the human body or to indicate and identify a room which provides such a facility.

Image content: Side view of showerhead with water indicated by lines of dots

Application: Buildings and other locations, floor plans, maps, guidebooks, orientation diagrams

Origin of example: ISO 7001

Tickets

Use: To indicate and identify a facility where tickets may be obtained. May be used for automatic distributors. Shall not be used to indicate a ticket check

Image content: Hand holding two tickets

Application: Buildings and other locations, floor plans, maps, guidebooks, orientation diagrams, vehicles

Origin of example: ISO 7001

Double Chairlift

Use: To inform the public that the chairlift can carry two passengers sitting side by side at the same time

Image content: Two human figures seated on a chair with attachment suspended from an inclined cable, in side view

Application: Ski and tourist resorts, sign boards, maps, guidebooks, orientation diagrams

Origin of example: ISO 7001

Triple Chairlift

Use: To inform the public that the chairlift can carry three passengers sitting side by side at the same time

Image content: Three human figures seated on a chair with attachment suspended from an inclined cable, in side view

Application: Ski and tourist resorts, sign boards, maps, guidebooks, orientation diagrams

Origin of example: ISO 7001

Quadruple Chairlift

Use: To inform the public that the chairlift can carry four passengers sitting side by side at the same time

Image content: Four human figures seated on a chair with attachment suspended from an inclined cable, in side view

Application: Ski and tourist resorts, sign boards, maps, guidebooks, orientation diagrams

Origin of example: ISO 7001

Line up four by four

Use: To instruct passengers to line up four by four

Image content: Four human figures drawn in solid form standing side by side in front view, behind each of which are similar figures drawn in outline

Application: Quadruple chair lifts, ski and tourist resorts, signboards, maps, and guidebooks

Origin of example: ISO 7001

Foot passengers have to get off

Use: To inform foot passengers on the chairlift of the location of the landing point for foot passengers

Image content: Human figure drawn in front of a suspended chair, in side view; an arrow indicates the required direction of movement

Application: Ski and tourist resorts, signboards, maps, and guidebooks

Origin of example: ISO 7001

Skiers have to get off

Use: To inform skiers on the chairlift of the location of the landing point for skiers

Image content: Human figure on skis drawn in front of a suspended chair, in side view; an arrow indicates the required direction of movement

Application: Ski and tourist resorts, signboards, maps, and guidebooks

Origin of example: ISO 7001

Steep-slope ski lift

Use: To inform skiers that parts of the track of the surface ski lift are steep

Image content: Human figure on skis drawn in side view; holding a rope, which is almost vertical. The skis are parallel to one side of a solid equilateral triangle with an inscribed % sign

Application: Ski and tourist resorts, signboards, maps, and guidebooks

Origin of example: ISO 7001

Old forms of transportation

Use: To indicate availability or presence of old forms of transport

Image content: Solid drawing of human figure sitting in line drawing of sleigh

Application: Ski and tourist resorts, signboards, maps, and guidebooks

Origin of example: Austria

High speed train

Use: To indicate and identify the location of a high speed train.

Image content: Various logos

Application: Buildings, public places, streets and roads, orientation diagrams, vehicles, rooms, corridors, etc.

Origin of examples: France, Belgium, UK

Underground station/Metro

Use: To indicate and identify the location of an underground or metro station.

Image content: Front view of an underground metro

Application: Buildings, public places, streets and roads, orientation diagrams, vehicles, rooms, corridors, etc.

Origin of example: IUC

Air strip

Use: To indicate and identify the location of an air strip.

Image content: Outline of a propeller plane

Application: Buildings, public places, streets and roads, orientation diagrams, vehicles, rooms, corridors, etc.

Origin of example: Argentina

Prayer place

Use: To indicate the availability of a prayer place

Image content: Side drawing of a figure bent in prayer before a line drawing of a cross

Application: Air and marine terminals and train stations

Origin of example: Bolivia

Seaport

Use: To indicate marine transport facilities

Image content: Side view drawing of a boat or ferry above two wavy lines attached to vertical line indicating the dock

Application: Seaports

Origin of example: Argentina

Cruise boat

Use: To indicate marine transport facilities
Image content: Angled drawing of a cruiser above two wavy lines alongside a strip indicating land with a palm tree
Application: Seaports
Origin of example: Portugal

Anchorage

Use: To indicate marine facilities for tourists
Image content: Graphic portrayal of an anchor in side view
Application: Harbours and seaside resorts
Origin of example: Portugal

Mooring point

Use: To indicate a mooring point available for tourists with boats
Image content: Side view drawing of a yacht on a line indicating the sea and a mooring point
Application: Harbours and seaside resorts
Origin of example: Portugal

Boat launching

Use: To indicate facilities for tourists to launch boats
Image content: Side view drawing of a boat on a trailer above two wavy lines indicating the water connected to wedge shape indicating land
Application: Tourism seaside resorts and waterside recreation areas
Origin of example: New Zealand

Tourist attractions

A. LIST OF REFERENTS

1. World Heritage attraction
2. Landmark
3. National park
4. National shrine
5. Unique monument
6. Nature reserve
7. Panorama/Look out/ Viewing point
8. Photography
9. Cave
10. Waterfall
11. Spa
12. Fountain
13. Cape/Peninsula
14. Botanical garden
15. Bird/Ornithological sanctuary
16. Endangered species sanctuary
17. Aquarium
18. Zoological garden
19. Trail with interpretation
20. Interpretation walk
21. Lighthouse
22. National Palace
23. House of Parliament
24. Historical monument
25. Religious monument (church)
26. Religious monument (mosque)
27. Religious monument (synagogue)
28. Religious monument (temple)
29. Castle
30. Monastery
31. Cloister
32. Historic water-mill
33. Prehistoric paintings or carvings
34. Prehistoric site
35. Urban centre
36. Cinema
37. Museum
38. Festivals
39. Folklore
40. Art gallery
41. Gastronomy
42. Vineyard
43. Markets and local fairs
44. Craft centre/Exhibit

B. DESCRIPTION OF REFERENTS

World Heritage attraction

Use: To indicate the location of a site or monument listed by UNESCO World Heritage (a list of 630 cultural and natural properties of outstanding universal value updated in December 1999. It consists of 480 cultural, 128 natural and 22 mixed properties in 118 States Parties)
Image content: Linear drawing of a circle limited to an open square
Application: Roads, street, outdoor recreation areas, maps, guidebooks, orientation diagrams
Origin of example: UNESCO
Comment: It may also be considered as a logo

Landmark

Use: To indicate the location of a landmark
Image content: In a circle, the stylized symbol of the country landmark
Application: Roads, outdoor recreation areas, maps, guidebooks, orientation diagrams
Origin of example: Chile

National park

Use: To indicate the location of a national park
Image content: Stylized tree or specific plant or animal silhouette best representing the preservation of fauna or flora
Application: Roads, outdoor recreation areas, maps, guidebooks, orientation diagrams
Origin of example: Chile

National shrine

Use: To indicate the location of a national shrine
Image content: Stylized silhouette representing the national shrine
Application: Roads, outdoor recreation areas, maps, guidebooks, orientation diagrams
Origin of example: Jordan

Unique monument

Use: To indicate the location of a national monument
Image content: Stylized drawing representing a unique monument
Application: Roads, outdoor recreation areas, maps, guidebooks, orientation diagrams
Origin of example: Jordan

Nature reserve

Use: To indicate the location of an area set aside for the preservation of flora and fauna
Image content: Tree silhouette alongside an appropriate animal
Application: Roads, outdoor recreation areas, maps, guidebooks, orientation diagrams
Origin of example: ISO 7001

Panorama/Look out/Viewing point

Use: To indicate a place or a point with an exceptional panoramic view
Image content: Eye with a bundle of rays
Application: Roads, outdoor recreation areas, maps, guidebooks, orientation diagrams
Origin of example: Israel

Photography

Use: To signify the activity of photography or a place where photo or movie camera shots can be done
Image content: Camera in front view
Application: Outdoor recreation areas, maps, guidebooks, orientation diagrams
Origin of example: Argentina

Cave

Use: To indicate the location of a cave
Image content: Linear drawing of a cave with human figure at the entrance
Application: Outdoor recreation areas, maps, guidebooks, orientation diagrams
Origin of example: Brazil

Waterfall

Use: To indicate the location of a waterfall
Image content: Linear drawing of a waterfall
Application: Outdoor recreation areas, maps, guidebooks, orientation diagrams
Origin of example: Brazil

Spa

Use: To indicate the location of a spa
Image content: Linear drawing of a spa fountain
Application: Outdoor recreation areas, maps, guidebooks, orientation diagrams
Origin of example: Romania

Fountain

Use: To indicate the location of a fountain
Image content: Linear drawing of a fountain
Application: Outdoor recreation areas, maps, guidebooks, orientation diagrams
Origin of example: Portugal

Cape/Peninsula

Use: To indicate the location of a cape or a peninsula
Image content: Linear drawing of a cape in side view
Application: Roads and motorways, outdoor recreation areas, maps, guidebooks, orientation diagrams
Origin of example: Portugal

Botanical garden

Use: To indicate the location of a botanical garden
Image content: Stylized silhouette of a unique flower
Application: Roads and motorways, outdoor recreation areas, maps, guidebooks, orientation diagrams
Origin of example: Belgium

Bird/Ornithological sanctuary

Use: To indicate the location of a bird sanctuary or an ornithological park
Image content: Bird (unique or endangered) in side view
Application: Roads and motorways, outdoor recreation areas, maps, guidebooks, orientation diagrams
Origin of example: Cyprus

Endangered species sanctuary

Use: To indicate a place where an endangered species can be found and to prevent drivers and people
Image content: Depends on the species
Application: Roads and motorways, outdoor recreation areas, maps, guidebooks, orientation diagrams
Origin of example: Thailand

Aquarium

Use: To indicate the location of an aquarium
Image content: Stylized fish in side view with some water bubbles
Application: Roads and motorways, outdoor recreation areas, maps, guidebooks, orientation diagrams
Origin of example: Portugal

Zoological garden

Use: To indicate the location of a zoological garden
Image content: ZOO in Latin letters is the most commonly used symbol
Application: Roads and motorways, outdoor recreation areas, maps, guidebooks, orientation diagrams
Origin of example: Portugal

Trail with interpretation

Use: To signify a walk for nature or heritage interpretation purposes
Image content: Rucksack or knapsack and cane with the letter "i"
Application: Outdoor recreation areas, maps, guidebooks, orientation diagrams
Origin of example: Austria

Interpretation walk

Use: To signify a walk for interpretation purposes
Image content: Walking human figure, tree's silhouette with letter "i" post
Application: Outdoor recreation areas, maps, guide-books, orientation diagrams
Origin of example: New Zealand

Lighthouse

Use: To indicate the location of a lighthouse of historical or technical interest
Image content: A linear drawing of lighthouse with bundle of rays
Application: Roads and motorways, outdoor recreation areas, maps, guidebooks, orientation diagrams
Origin of example: Turkey

National Palace

Use: To indicate the location of the Palace of the Head of State
Image content: A linear drawing in front view of a palace
Application: Roads and motorways, urban centres, maps, guidebooks, orientation diagrams
Origin of example: Austria

House of Parliament

Use: To indicate the location of the House of the Parliament of the Nation
Image content: A linear drawing in front view of a Parliament House with columns
Application: Roads and motorways, urban centres, maps, guidebooks, orientation diagrams
Origin of example: Argentina

Historical monument

Use: To indicate the location of a monument of historical importance
Image content: A linear drawing in front view of temple (most commonly used)
Application: Roads and motorways, urban centres, maps, guidebooks, orientation diagrams
Origin of example: Iraq

Religious monument (church)

Use: To indicate the location of a religious monument, shrine or building where it is possible to pray and to follow the observance of the Christian religion

Image content: A shelter above a cross on a plain strip

Application: Roads and motorways, urban centres, maps, guidebooks, orientation diagrams

Origin of example: Thailand

Religious monument (mosque)

Use: To indicate the location of a religious monument, shrine or building where it is possible to pray and to follow the observance of the Moslem religion

Image content: A shelter above a crescent on a plain strip

Application: Roads and motorways, urban centres, maps, guidebooks, orientation diagrams

Origin of example: Thailand

Religious monument (synagogue)

Use: To indicate the location of a religious monument, shrine or building where it is possible to pray and to follow the observance of the Jewish religion

Image content: The Star of David on synagogue motif.

Application: Roads and motorways, urban centres, maps, guidebooks, orientation diagrams

Origin of example: Israel

Religious monument (temple)

Use: To indicate the location of a religious monument, shrine or building where it is possible to pray and to follow the observance of the Buddhist religion

Image content: A shelter above a wheel on a plain strip

Application: Roads and motorways, urban centres, maps, guidebooks, orientation diagrams

Origin of example: Thailand

Castle

Use: To indicate the location of an ancient castle

Image content: A linear drawing a castle's tower from the Middle Ages

Application: Roads and motorways, maps, guidebooks, orientation diagrams

Origin of example: The Netherlands

Monastery

Use: To indicate the location of a monastery

Image content: Linear drawing of a monastery stylized according to the national or local architecture

Application: Roads and motorways, urban centres, maps, guidebooks, orientation diagrams

Origin of example: Cyprus

Cloister

Use: To indicate the location of a cloister

Image content: Four arches and columns representing an angle of a cloister stylized according to the national or local architecture

Application: Roads and motorways, urban centres, maps, guidebooks, orientation diagrams

Origin of example: Portugal

Historic water mill

Use: To indicate the location of a historic water mill

Image content: Water mill wheel linear drawing in side view and a house in background

Application: Roads and motorways, maps, guidebooks, orientation diagrams

Origin of example: Portugal

Prehistoric paintings or carvings

Use: To indicate a place where prehistoric or archaic paintings or carvings can be seen

Image content: Hands, marks and naive drawing of human figures and animals

Application: Roads and motorways, outdoor recreation areas, maps, guidebooks, orientation diagrams

Origin of example: Argentina

Prehistoric site

Use: To indicate the location of a prehistoric site
Image content: Mark depending on the site
Application: Roads and motorways, outdoor recreation areas,
maps, guidebooks, orientation diagrams
Origin of example: Columbia

Urban centre

Use: To indicate and orient towards a city centre
Image content: Three circles with a plain centre point
Application: Roads and motorways, maps, guidebooks, ori-
entation diagrams
Origin of example: Portugal

Cinema

Use: To indicate the location of a movie theater
Image content: Three persons in front of a strip depicting c piece of film
Application: Public places, orientation diagrams, maps
Origin of example: China GB 10001-94/62

Museums

Use: To indicate the location of a museum
Image content: Different possible symbols depending on the national or local culture and civilization
Application: Roads and motorways, public places, orientation diagrams, maps, guidebooks
Origin of example: U.K. (an object under a shelter)

Festivals

Use: To signify the existence of festival events
Image content: Dancers or actors on a theatre stage
Application: Guidebooks, Orientation maps
Origin of example: Iraq

Folklore

Use: To indicate the location of a place where regional or national folklore can be found
Image content: A dancing couple in front of a historic monument
Application: Roads and motorways, Outdoor recreation areas, orientation diagrams, maps, guidebooks
Origin of example: Portugal

Art gallery

Use: To indicate the location of an art gallery
Image content: A symbolic drawing of a painting or a sculpture near a human figure
Application: Public places, orientation diagrams, maps, guidebooks
Origin of example: Bolivia

Gastronomy

Use: To indicate the location of a gastronomical centre or restaurant

Image content: A symbolic drawing of the local or national food specialties

Application: Public places, orientation diagrams, maps, guidebooks

Origin of example: Portugal

Vineyard

Use: To indicate the location of a vineyard or a wine centre

Image content: A symbolic drawing of a bunch of grapes

Application: Public places, orientation diagrams, maps, guidebooks

Origin of example: Portugal

Markets and local fairs

Use: To indicate the location of a typical market or a local fair

Image content: A symbolic drawing of a market or fair

Application: Public places, orientation diagrams, maps, guidebooks

Origin of example: Iraq

Craft centre/Exhibit

Use: To indicate the location of a craft centre or exhibit

Image content: A symbolic drawing of potters' art or other local or national specific craftsmanship

Application: Public places, orientation diagrams, maps, guidebooks

Origin of example: Ghana

Sports and outdoor recreation

A. LIST OF REFERENTS

1. Sporting activities
2. Facilities for sport
3. Gymnasium/Fitness centre
4. Motor-racing track
5. Four-wheel-drive routes
6. Shelter
7. Walking track/Path
8. Trekking
9. Route
10. Barbecue
11. Archery
12. Athletic events
13. Ballooning
14. Basketball
15. Billiards
16. Bowling
17. Boxing
18. Eurhythmics
19. Fencing
20. Football
21. No football
22. Handball
23. Judo
24. Karate
25. Wrestling
26. Rugby
27. Indoor volleyball
28. Weight lifting
29. Bull fighting
30. Boating
31. Boat hire
32. Canoeing
33. Rowing
34. Rafting

35. Caving
36. Climbing
37. Cycling
38. Bicycle hire
39. Mountain biking
40. Trial bike riding
41. Diving
42. Scuba diving
43. Fishing
44. River fishing
45. Boat fishing
46. Shellfish gathering
47. Geology
48. Gold panning
49. Golf
50. Hang gliding
51. Paragliding
52. Parachuting
53. Horse riding
54. Polo
55. Hippodrome / Race course
56. Hunting / Shooting
57. Small game
58. Game bird hunting
59. Clay pigeon shooting
60. Ice-skating
61. Jogging
62. Mini-golf / Croquet
63. Orienteering
64. Downhill skiing
65. Ski touring
66. Snowboarding
67. Tobogganing
68. Swimming

69. Water-skiing
70. Surfing
71. Windsurfing
72. Jet skiing
73. Aquatic park
74. Tennis
75. Squash / Racket ball
76. Table tennis
77. Do not feed birds or animals
78. Do not remove vegetation

B. DESCRIPTION OF REFERENTS

Sporting activities

Use: To indicate and identify the location of an area set side for sporting activities
Image content: Three distinct items of sports equipment
Application: Buildings, services, public places, maps, guidebooks, orientation diagrams
Origin of example: ISO 7001

Facilities for sport

Use: To indicate the location of facilities for sports or a sport field
Image content: Five Olympic circles
Application: Outdoor recreation areas, services, public places, maps, guidebooks, orientation diagrams
Origin of example: China (Macao)
Comments: This symbol looks like the Olympic logotype and is used in many destinations

Gymnasium/Fitness centre

Use: To indicate the location of a gymnasium or a fitness centre or a place where gymnastics or fitness can be exercised
Image content: Human figure exercising with heavy weights or dumbbells
Application: Outdoor recreation areas, buildings, services, public places, maps, guidebooks, orientation diagrams
Origin of example: China

Motor-racing track

Use: To indicate the location of a motor-racing track
Image content: Race car and pilot in side view
Application: Outdoor recreation areas, services, public places, maps, guidebooks, orientation diagrams
Origin of example: China (Macao)

Four wheel drive routes

Use: To indicate the road is suitable only for four wheel drive vehicles

Image content: Vehicle in side view climbing a bumpy slope with the mark 4x4

Application: Outdoor recreation areas, roads and trails, maps, guidebooks, orientation diagrams

Origin of example: New Zealand

Shelter

Use: To indicate a facility that provides temporary /emergency shelter

Image content: Human figure under a stylised shelter (^)

Application: Outdoor recreation areas, roads and trails, maps, guidebooks, orientation diagrams

Origin of example: New Zealand

Walking track/Path

Use: To signify a path classification track, trail or path or the activity of walking

Image content: Adult and child human figures walking

Application: Outdoor recreation areas, roads and trails, maps, guidebooks, orientation diagrams

Origin of example: New Zealand

Comment: A strip on the down side of the square can be added with the following colours:

Green: Easy

Yellow: Moderate

Red: Difficult

Black: Dangerous or dangerous portion of the path

Trekking

Use: To signify a trek or tramping classification trail /track or the activity

Image content: Human figure trekking with a rucksack

Application: Outdoor recreation areas, roads and trails, maps, guidebooks, orientation diagrams

Origin of example: New Zealand (tramping track)

Comment: A strip on the down side of the square can be added with the following colours:

Green: Easy
Yellow: Moderate
Red: Difficult
Black: Dangerous or dangerous portion of the path

Route

Use: To signify a route classification track
Image content: Human figure walking uphill on a bumpy track with a rucksack
Application: Outdoor recreation areas, roads and trails, maps, guidebooks, orientation diagrams
Origin of example: New Zealand
Comment: A strip on the down side of the square can be added with the following colours:
Green: Easy
Yellow: Moderate
Red: Difficult
Black: Dangerous or dangerous portion of the route

Barbecue

Use: To signify barbecue facilities
Image content: Stylised fork with sausage above a ground fire
Application: Outdoor recreation areas, orientation diagrams
Origin of example: New Zealand

Ballooning

Use: To signify and indicate the location of ballooning activities and facilities
Image content: Linear drawing of an old balloon (Montgolfiere)
Application: Outdoor recreation areas, orientation diagrams
Origin of example: Portugal

Billiards

Use: To signify and indicate the location of activities and facilities for billiards
Image content: Human figure playing billiards
Application: Buildings, public places, outdoor recreation areas, orientation diagrams, and guidebooks
Origin of example: China

Bowling

Use: To signify and indicate the location of activities and facilities for bowling
Image content: Linear drawing of a bowl and a set of skittles
Application: Buildings, public places, outdoor recreation areas, orientation diagrams, and guidebooks
Origin of example: China

Bull fighting

Use: To signify and indicate the location of bullfighting facilities and plays
Image content: Toreador's figure in front view with cape and bull silhouette in side view
Application: Public places, roads and motorways, orientation diagrams, maps and guidebooks
Origin of example: Portugal

Boating

Use: To indicate boating as outdoor recreation activity
Image content: Human figure in motor boat in side view
Application: Outdoor recreation areas, public places, maps, guidebooks, orientation diagrams
Origin of example: Argentina

Boat hire

Use: To indicate and identify a location where recreational boats can be hired
Image content: Motor boat figure under key in side view
Application: Outdoor recreation areas, public places, maps, guidebooks, orientation diagrams
Origin of example: Spain

Canoeing

Use: To indicate a canoe and identify a location for canoeing activity
Image content: Human figure canoeing above two wavy lines
Application: Outdoor recreation areas, maps, guidebooks, orientation diagrams
Origin of example: New Zealand

Rafting

Use: To signify a raft and identify a location for the activity of rafting

Image content: Raft linear drawing with three human figures going down above two wavy lines

Application: Outdoor recreation areas, maps, guidebooks, orientation diagrams

Origin of example: New Zealand

Caving

Use: To signify the activity of caving

Image content: Human figure kneeling down in a cave with front lighting in side view

Application: Outdoor recreation areas, maps, guidebooks, orientation diagrams

Origin of example: New Zealand

Climbing

Use: To signify the activity of climbing or mountain climbing

Image content: Human figure kneeling down in a cave with front lighting in side view

Application: Outdoor recreation areas, maps, guidebooks, orientation diagrams

Origin of example: New Zealand

Comment: A strip on the down side of the square can be added with the following colours:

Green: Easy
Yellow: Moderate
Red: Difficult
Black: Dangerous

Cycling

Use: To indicate and identify a location for cycling activity

Image content: Human figure on bicycle in side view

Application: Outdoor recreation areas, street and roads, guidebooks, orientation maps

Origin of example: New Zealand

Bicycle hire

Use: To indicate and identify a location where bicycles and other cycles can be hire

Image content: Bicycle in side view

Application: Outdoor recreation areas, street and roads, guidebooks, orientation maps

Origin of example: Austria

Mountain biking

Use: To indicate and identify a location for mountain biking activity

Image content: Human figure on mountain bike in side view

Application: Outdoor recreation areas, guidebooks, orientation maps

Origin of example: Austria

Comment: A strip on the down side of the square can be added with the following colours:

Green: Easy
Yellow: Moderate
Red: Difficult
Black: Dangerous

Trial bike riding

Use: To indicate and identify a location for trial bike riding activity

Image content: Human figure on trial bike in side view on a bumpy trail up

Application: Outdoor recreation areas, guidebooks, orientation maps

Origin of example: New Zealand

Comment: A strip on the down side of the square can be added with the following colours:

Green: Easy
Yellow: Moderate
Red: Difficult
Black: Dangerous

Diving

Use: To signify the activity of diving
Image content: Human figure starting to dive above two wavy lines
Application: Outdoor recreation areas, maps, guidebooks, orientation diagrams
Origin of example: New Zealand

Scuba diving

Use: To signify the activity of scuba diving
Image content: Human figure of scuba diver with bottle and some bubbles up
Application: Outdoor recreation areas, maps, guidebooks, orientation diagrams
Origin of example: New Zealand
Comments:
1. The Argentinean variant has an image content of a scuba diver figure under two wavy lines
2. A strip on the down side of the square can be added with the following colours:
   Green: No danger
   Black: Dangerous

Fishing

Use: To signify the activity of fishing
Image content: Human figure angling above two wavy lines
Application: Outdoor recreation areas, maps, guidebooks, orientation diagrams
Origin of example: New Zealand

River fishing

Use: To signify the activity of river fishing
Image content: Human figure of fisherman with angle and fish above two wavy lines
Application: Outdoor recreation areas, maps, guidebooks, orientation diagrams
Origin of example: Austria

Boat fishing

Use: To signify the activity of fishing from a boat
Image content: Human figure of fisherman with angle on a small boat above two wavy lines
Application: Outdoor recreation areas, maps, guidebooks, orientation diagrams
Origin of example: New Zealand

Shellfish gathering

Use: To signify the activity of shellfish gathering
Image content: A hand grasping a shellfish above two wavy lines
Application: Outdoor recreation areas, maps, guidebooks, orientation diagrams
Origin of example: New Zealand

Football

Use: To signify the possibility of football as an outdoor recreation activity
Image content: Human figure with a ball under feet
Application: Outdoor recreation areas, maps, guidebooks, orientation diagrams
Origin of example: Austria

No Football

Use: To signify the prohibition of football
Image content: Human figure with a ball under feet with a prohibition red slash
Application: Outdoor recreation areas, maps, guidebooks, orientation diagrams
Origin of example: Austria

Geology

Use: To signify the possibility of geology as an outdoor recreation activity
Image content: Pickaxe and three small stones in side view
Application: Outdoor recreation areas, maps, guidebooks, orientation diagrams
Origin of example: New Zealand

Gold panning

Use: To signify the possibility of gold panning as an outdoor recreation activity

Image content: Human figure with gold pan above two wavy lines

Application: Outdoor recreation areas, maps, guidebooks, orientation diagrams

Origin of example: New Zealand

Golf

Use: To indicate the possibility of golf or a golf course

Image content: Human figure swinging a club

Application: Outdoor recreation, roads and motorways, maps, guidebooks, orientation diagrams

Origin of example: China

Hang gliding

Use: To signify the possibility and locate a facility for hang gliding

Image content: Human figure under a delta glide

Application: Outdoor recreation areas, maps, guidebooks, orientation diagrams

Origin of example: New Zealand

Paragliding

Use: To signify the possibility and locate a facility for paragliding

Image content: Human figure under a paraglide and a rope attached

Application: Outdoor recreation areas, maps, guidebooks, orientation diagrams

Origin of example: New Zealand

Parachuting

Use: To signify the possibility and locate a facility for parachuting

Image content: Human figure under a parachute

Application: Outdoor recreation areas, maps, guidebooks, orientation diagrams

Origin of example: New Zealand

Horse riding

Use: To signify the possibility and locate a facility for horse riding

Image content: Human figure on horse

Application: Outdoor recreation areas, roads and trails, maps, guidebooks, orientation diagrams

Origin of example: Austria

Comments: Variants can exist with a slash for prohibition or under a shelter to locate a indoor activity

Polo

Use: To signify the activity of polo and locate a polo field

Image content: Human figure on horse with polo club in side view

Application: Outdoor recreation areas, roads and trails, maps, guidebooks, orientation diagrams

Origin of example: Argentina

Hippodrome/Race course

Use: To indicate the location of a horse-race field

Image content: Horse and cavalier in side view

Application: Roads and public places, maps, guidebooks, orientation diagrams

Origin of example: China (Macao)

Hunting/Shooting

Use: To indicate the possibility and an outdoor area for hunting or shooting

Image content: Human figure shooting with gun

Application: Outdoor recreation areas, maps, guidebooks, orientation diagrams

Origin of example: Mexico

Small game

Use: To indicate the possibility and an outdoor area for hunting small game

Image content: Rabbit or hare silhouette running

Application: Outdoor recreation areas, maps, guidebooks, orientation diagrams

Origin of example: Spain

Game bird hunting

Use: To indicate the possibility and an outdoor area for hunting game bird

Image content: Human figure shooting bird

Application: Outdoor recreation areas, maps, guidebooks, orientation diagrams

Origin of example: New Zealand

Clay pigeon shooting

Use: To indicate the possibility and an outdoor area for shooting clay pigeon

Image content: Human figure shooting and clay plate above

Application: Outdoor recreation areas, maps, guidebooks, orientation diagrams

Origin of example: Portugal

Ice-skating

Use: To signify the activity of ice-skating

Image content: Human figure ice skating in side view

Application: Outdoor recreation areas, maps, guidebooks, orientation diagrams

Origin of example: New Zealand

Comment: A variant exists for indoor ice-skating; same image content under shelter ^

Jogging

Use: To signify the possibility of jogging or the location of a jogging path

Image content: Human figure jogging

Application: Outdoor recreation areas , street and roads, maps, guidebooks, orientation diagrams

Origin of example: New Zealand

Comment: The Chinese variant shows a linear drawing of a path with directional arrow

Mini-golf/Croquet

Use: To signify the possibility of mini-golf or croquet and indicate the location of a mini-golf or croquet facility
Image content: Human figure with club, croquet hoop and croquet ball
Application: Outdoor recreation areas, street and public places, maps, guidebooks, orientation diagrams
Origin of example: Austria

Orienteering

Use: To signify the activity of orienteering
Image content: Human figure jogging within a circle showing North (N), West (W) and East (E)
Application: Outdoor recreation areas, maps, guidebooks, orientation diagrams
Origin of example: New Zealand

Rowing

Use: To signify the possibility of rowing
Image content: Human figure rowing in a rowing boat in side view above two wavy lines
Application: Outdoor recreation areas, maps, guidebooks, orientation diagrams
Origin of example: Argentina
Comment: A variant exists to prohibit rowing with the same image content and red slash

Rugby

Use: To signify the possibility of rugby
Image content: Human figure running with a rugby ball
Application: Outdoor recreation areas, maps, guidebooks, orientation diagrams
Origin of example: Argentina

Downhill skiing

Use: To signify the activity of downhill skiing and to locate a ski slope
Image content: Human figure downhill skiing with skis in side view
Application: Ski and tourist resorts, sign boards, maps, guide-

books, orientation diagrams

Origin of example: Austria

Comment: A strip on the down side of the square can be added with the following colours:

Green: Easy

Yellow: Moderate

Red: Difficult

Black: Dangerous

A variant exists to prohibit downhill with the same image content and red slash.

Ski touring

Use: To signify the activity of ski touring and to locate a ski touring trail

Image content: Human figure with skis in side view

Application: Ski and tourist resorts, sign boards, maps, guidebooks, orientation diagrams

Origin of example: Austria

Comment: A strip on the down side of the square can be added with the following colours:

Green: Easy

Yellow: Moderate

Red: Difficult

Black: Dangerous

A variant exists to prohibit ski touring with the same image content and red slash.

Snowboarding

Use: To signify the activity of snowboarding and to locate a snowboarding slope

Image content: Human figure with snowboard

Application: Ski and tourist resorts, sign boards, maps, guidebooks, orientation diagrams

Origin of example: Austria

Comment: A strip on the down side of the square can be added with the following colours:

Green: Easy

Yellow: Moderate

Red: Difficult

A variant exists to prohibit snowboarding with the same image content and red slash.

Tobogganing

Use: To signify the activity of tobogganing and to locate a tobogganing facility

Image content: Human figure seated on a tobogganing ski

Application: Ski and tourist resorts, sign boards, maps, guidebooks, orientation diagrams

Origin of example: New Zealand

Comment: A strip on the down side of the square can be added with the following colours:

Green: Easy
Yellow: Moderate
Red: Difficult
Black: Dangerous

A variant exists to prohibit tobogganing with the same image content and red slash.

Swimming

Use: To signify the possibility of swimming and to locate beaches and other swimming facilities

Image content: Human torso drawn swimming above two wavy lines

Application: Outdoor recreation areas, roads and trails, maps, guidebooks, orientation diagrams

Origin of example: Argentina

Comment: A coloured beach warning flag can be added:

Green for safe
Yellow or orange for caution
Red for dangerous/Unsafe

A variant exists to prohibit swimming with the same image content and red slash.

Water-skiing

Use: To signify the possibility of water-skiing and to locate beaches and other facilities for water-skiing

Image content: Human figure water-skiing above two wavy lines in side view

Application: Outdoor recreation areas, roads and trails, maps, guidebooks, orientation diagrams
Origin of example: Argentina
Comment: A coloured beach warning flag can be added:
Green for safe
Yellow or orange for caution
Red for dangerous/Unsafe
A variant exists to prohibit swimming with the same image content and red slash.

Surfing

Use: To signify the possibility of surfing and to locate beaches and other facilities for surfing
Image content: Human figure and surfboard above wavy lines
Application: Outdoor recreation areas, roads and trails, maps, guidebooks, orientation diagrams
Origin of example: Portugal
Comment: A coloured beach warning flag can be added:
Green for safe
Yellow or orange for caution
Red for dangerous/Unsafe
A variant exists to prohibit swimming with the same image content and red slash.

Windsurfing

Use: To signify the possibility of windsurfing and to locate beaches and other facilities for windsurfing
Image content: Human figure and windsurf sail above two wavy lines
Application: Outdoor recreation areas, roads and trails, maps, guidebooks, orientation diagrams
Origin of example: Austria
Comment: A coloured beach warning flag can be added:
Green for safe
Yellow or orange for caution
Red for dangerous/Unsafe
A variant exists to prohibit swimming with the same image content and red slash.

Jet skiing

Use: To signify the possibility of jet skiing and to locate beaches and other facilities for jet skiing
Image content: Human figure on Jet Ski in side view above two wavy lines
Application: Outdoor recreation areas, roads and trails, maps, guidebooks, orientation diagrams
Origin of example: Argentina
Comment: A coloured beach warning flag can be added:
Green for safe
Yellow or orange for caution
Red for dangerous/Unsafe
A variant exists to prohibit swimming with the same image content and red slash.

Aquatic park

Use: To indicate the location of an aquatic park
Image content: Human figure on water toboggan and seal silhouette playing with a ball in side view
Application: Outdoor recreation, maps, guidebooks, orientation diagrams
Origin of example: Portugal

Tennis

Use: To indicate and identify a facility for playing tennis or tennis courts.
Image content: Human figure with racket and ball, with horizontal double line representing the top of the net
Application: Buildings and other locations, maps, guidebooks, orientation diagrams
Origin of example: ISO 7001

Squash/Racket ball

Use: To indicate and identify a facility for playing squash and/or racket ball
Image content: Lines representing the corner of a room, with superimposed human figure holding a racket above which is a ball. For small-scale reproduction the ball may be omitted
Application: Buildings and other locations, maps, guidebooks, orientation diagrams
Origin of example: ISO 7001

Table tennis

Use: To signify the possibility of table tennis
Image content: Linear drawing of a table tennis racket and ball
Application: Outdoor recreation, maps, guidebooks, orientation diagrams
Origin of example: China
Comment: A variant may exist to prohibit this activity with the same image content and red slash.

Do not feed birds or animals

Use: To indicate feeding birds or animals is not permitted
Image content: Human hand feeding bird silhouette and diagonal red slash
Application: Outdoor recreation, maps, guidebooks, orientation diagrams
Origin of example: New Zealand (in this case, the bird is a kea)
Comment: Variants may exist with other bird or animal silhouette depending on the location

Do not remove vegetation

Use: To indicate that the removal of vegetation is not permitted
Image content: Human hand close to a plant with three leaves or petals and diagonal red slash
Application: Outdoor recreation, maps, guidebooks, orientation diagrams
Origin of example: New Zealand
Comment: Variants may exist with different or specific plants depending on the site, edelweiss for example in the Alpine countries.

Typical icons found in Internet portals and Web sites for travel information and electronic commerce[1]

Air Car Hotel

Vacations Cruises Specials

[1] Source: Yahoo! Travel Portal, March 2001.

Relationship between the Thesaurus on Tourism and Leisure Activities, graphical symbols and internet icons

In 2000, the World Tourism Organization, in cooperation with the Secretariat of State for Tourism of France, published a trilingual (from French to English to Spanish) *Thesaurus on Tourism and Leisure Activities*. Its relationship with graphical symbols and icons can soon be established, in the latter case thanks to the development and rapid use of new information and communication technologies.

The basic framework of the *Thesaurus* is made up of semantic areas which include terms, definitions and relations linking the terms to each other. The semantic areas are the following:

01. Sports	11. Tourism Heritage
02. Tourism Legislation	12. Tourism Policy
03. Ecology of Tourism	13. Tourism Services
04. Economy of Tourism	14. Tourism Professionals
05. Tourism Facilities	15. Tourism Promotion
06. Visitor Flows	16. Science and Information
07. Training and Employment	17. Sociology of Leisure
08. Accommodation	18. Tourism Sectors
09. Leisure Activities	19. Transport
10. Tourism Events	20. Countries and Country Groupings

Accordingly, the structure of catalogues, inventories, search engines and portals in the internet could follow on the relevant parts of the Thesaurus (shown in bold type in the list above) to which graphical symbols or icons could be attributed.

2. GUIDANCE FOR THE USE OF SYMBOLS

Acceptance and confusion

According to ISO principles, a symbol is reliable when it is tested with more than 85 % criteria for acceptance and no more than 5% critical confusion answers. In particular, safety signs must be rigorously examined for the quality of the graphical representation and for the ability of the visitor audience to understand with confidence the intended message.

Graphic and overall design considerations[1]

It is necessary that the graphic design of symbols and markers meet specific criteria to transmit information in an optimum way. As quoted from ANSI, the American National Standards Institute, "individual symbols should be designed, wherever possible, as elements of a consistent visual system", i.e. according to rules such as:

Proportion: avoid long, narrow forms.

Symmetry: generally, symbols should be designed to be symmetrical about a vertical or horizontal axis.

Direction: conflicts or ambiguities in direction must be avoided. When a symbol with directional characteristics is combined with another directional element, the combination shall give the same directional information.

Form: solid forms are preferred to outline forms. An outline form, if used, should be bold and discriminated from its background.

Detail: simple geometric forms are preferred. The use of superfluous detail or decoration shall be avoided the critical details of the symbols should be able to be discriminated at the intended viewing distance.

Size: since symbols may be used on large and small areas, objects or documents, they should be legible at the intended viewing distance.

Placement: especially for safety signs, which should be placed within the normal field of view, and near the hazard or area for which action is required.

Environment: attention should be paid to environmental factors such as dirt, degradation, light level and light quality which may impair the effectiveness of a symbol.

Composite signs: sometimes they create more problems than solutions. It is better in strategic locations of attraction-rich areas to use information bays with maps and other signs with their explanation.

Colours (from the Convention on Roads Signs and Signals)

- All destination signs are generally coloured white on a green background.

- Safety signs are generally red or black and white.

- Tourist signs generally have white borders and worded legends on brown backgrounds.

- Outdoor recreation signs and posts have generally dark green background colours.

- Information and service signs are generally coloured white on dark blue background.

- Generally Matt finished colours are preferred over high gloss, but either may be used. Gloss and Matt finishes look quite different so the choice should be used consistently within a locality.

Dimensions

Dimensions depend on the purpose and the location of the symbol. The Convention on Road Signs and Signals indicates that "signs shall be so placed that they do not obstruct vehicular traffic on the carriageway, and, if placed on the verges, obstruct pedestrians as little as possible and that the dimensions of sign panels shall be such that the sign is easily visible from a distance and can be easily understood by a person approaching it" (according to the maximum speed allowed of his/her vehicle for example). Further, as a general rule the Convention indicates that there shall be four sizes for each type of sign:

- small signs where conditions do not permit the use of normal signs or where traffic can only move slowly (but no less than 0.60 m for the side of a danger warning, a mandatory or a regulatory sign),

- normal size (for example, the normal size of a danger warning, a mandatory or a regulatory sign shall measure approximately 0.90m),

- large size where very wide roads carry high-speed traffic,

- very large signs on roads carrying very high-speed traffic, such as motorways[2].

Shape

Generally, also according to the Convention, the shape depends on the type of signage. The commonly accepted standards are the following:

- advance signs are rectangular in shape and having their long axis horizontal,
- position signs have a chevron direction indicator and one end shaped as a point[3],
- advance warning signs are generally rectangular

The Convention also reminds that:

- signs prohibiting or restricting standing or parking shall be circular,

- signs providing useful information on parking shall be square,

- danger warning signs are equilateral triangles or squares with one diagonal vertical,

- signs regulating priority at intersections, danger warning signs at approaches to intersections and signs regulating priority on narrow sections of road may be:
  - equilateral triangle,
  - octagonal,
  - circular,
  - square with one diagonal vertical,
  - mandatory signs shall be circular,

- informative signs are usually rectangular; however, direction signs may be in the shape of an elongated rectangle with the longer side horizontal, terminating in an arrowhead.

Consistent use of symbols

As pointed out in the "APEC strategy":

- the more a symbol is used, the more familiar it becomes,

- introducing needless differences confuses the visitor and undermines the effectiveness of symbols,

- tourists/visitors faced with a growing number of symbols, the fewer they have to remember the better.

Use in travel literature

"Remember, target by design: if I can't read your material, you might as well have not spent the money to create it."
(Hal Norvell, AARP)

In travel literature (maps, brochures, etc.), the dimension of signs and symbols depends on the graphic context. A very common error is to consider the use of graphical symbols only from the viewpoint of design and aesthetics while neglecting the practical aspect of visually distinguishing their image content. For example, in travel catalogues and guides, the size of symbols may be too small or they may be reproduced against a dark background, so it will make the page look attractive, but not easy or even impossible to read and understand. Annex 6 explains how print communication (including graphic symbols) should be organized to target the mature reader or senior traveller.

[1] From APEC, Standardization of Symbols for Visitor Signage, Final Report, Singapore, May 1999.

[2] In some APEC member economies, these dimensions have been defined. The Signs Manual of Transit New Zealand proposes two sizes for all tourist signs A and B.
The A size signs shall be used when:
the speed of approaching vehicles is less than 70 km/h,
the sign is not affected by competing visual stimuli, and
the sign is not offset too far from a driver's normal line of sight.
The B size signs shall be used in all other situations.

[3] In New Zealand, for example, it is proposed that "when the direction is not indicated at right angles to the main road, the narrower rectangular type of sign with an arrow direction indicator should be used."

CHAPTER IV

GRAPHIC SYMBOLS USED IN TOURISM AS LOGOTYPES

In addition to tourism signs and symbols used for public and visitor information, the tourism sector is witness to an increasing number of logotypes (logos) which serve as distinguishing emblems or devices for organizations, companies, products, campaigns, programmes, destinations or even countries. They are commonly displayed in advertising material, official head letter paper and accessories associated with the promotion of tourism or its specific objectives (merchandising). The use of logotypes implies to be subject to juridical, administrative and operational considerations and procedures which may be fixed by national or even international law.

Some logotypes may have a labelling function (which has to be compatible with label content), in order to identify companies and organizations following a pattern of criteria, certified or not, within a specific programme such as aimed at ethics, ecology, safety and security, health and hygiene, etc.

For the purpose of this chapter, logotypes can be assembled in six broad groups relating to:

- special campaigns or programmes
- routes
- destinations (including countries)
- trademarks
- special events
- quality labels

1. SPECIAL CAMPAIGNS OR PROGRAMMES

National and international campaigns and special programmes are frequent in tourism to mobilize the public, defend determined values, warn against certain risks or attitudes, and induce positive or correct behaviour. The use of a logotype can help strengthen the public image of a special activity, provide for self-identification of their participants or call attention to the object of the campaign or programme. As a rule, everyone using such logos should develop a specific action, policy, professional code of conduct and other self-regulatory measures conforming to the aims of the campaign or programme.

Following are examples of international campaigns or programmes such as NO CHILD SEX TOURISM, THE BLUE FLAG, THE GREEN GLOBE and TUTTO for which logos have been used.

NO CHILD SEX TOURISM

Origin

Originally used by the Brazilian Tourist Board (EMBRATUR) in the national campaign, the logo was adopted for an international campaign in 1997 by the Child Prostitution and Tourism Task Force composed of tourism industry groups, non-governmental organizations and the World Tourism Organization (WTO). It is displayed in the Internet page of the Child Prostitution and Tourism Watch under the WTO home page (www.world-tourism.org).

Function

- to identify organizations, companies and establishments actively working to prevent and eliminate child prostitution;
- to sensitize the staff concerned;
- to inform travellers, the users of tourism establishments and the public at large of the campaign.

Image content

Application

Travel catalogues, advice for travellers (brochures), window displays, accommodation establishments, suitcases (stickers, tags), in-flight magazines, in-flight videos, etc.

The logo can be accompanied by any other logo, sign, graphic or public information symbol or message to identify the organization using the international logo and to transmit the organization's own message.

THE BLUE FLAG

Origin

The Blue Flag campaign organized by the Foundation for Environmental Education in Europe (FEEE) began in the mid-1980s as a means of encouraging local authorities to provide clean and safe beaches and marinas for local populations and tourists. The campaign was increasingly conducted within the much wider context of environmental improvement of the coastal area, and the criteria used in the campaign have been progressively broadened as the campaign has matured.

Function

The Blue Flag is an annual award scheme (sometimes considered as eco-label) that seeks to reward local governments and its partners for providing safe and clean coastal areas. It is linked with 12 signs to express criteria for beach management and safety (see previous Chapter II).

Image content

Application

Flying the Blue Flag on awarded beaches and marinas, or displaying it on travel catalogues, brochures, orientation diagrams, maps, etc.

GREEN GLOBE

Origin
The Green Globe is a world-wide environmental programme for the travel and tourism industry. Started in 1994, the Green Globe is a follow up to the 1992 Rio Earth Summit, the UN Conference on Environment and Development, and the strategic outlook at the implications of Agenda 21 for Tourism taken by the Earth Council, the World Travel and Tourism Council and the World Tourism Organization.

Function
The Green Globe is recognized as an ecobrand in environmental and mainstream tourism. The logotype is limited to a specific certification programme through which a company can show, through independent assessment, that it is addressing issues of environmental, social and cultural responsibility.

Image content

Application
Establishments, travel catalogues, brochures, window displays, etc.

TUTTO

Function

The international project "TOURISM FOR ALL" under the motto "TUTTO"1 is dedicated to improve access to tourism facilities equipment and services for people with disabilities of any kind, without pointing out any specific disability (See Annex 5).

Image content

Application

The logotype can be used in establishments, travel catalogues, brochures, window displays, etc.

2. INTERNATIONAL TOURIST ROUTES

In 1960 the Council of Europe stressed the importance of cultural travel as a quality way of using leisure time. In 1985, also, WTO called for the development of new tourism products to facilitate encounters among people and indicated that such products could be built around important tourist routes.

Following the Council of Europe initiative, the European cultural itineraries were launched in 1987 with three main objectives:

- to make the common cultural identity more visible, to enhance it and encourage the citizens of Europe to share it,
- to safeguard and enhance the European cultural heritage as a way of improving lifestyle and as a source of social, economic and cultural development,
- to give citizens new possibilities of fulfilment by focusing on cultural tourism and related activities.

Many projects have been put in place: the Roads to Santiago, the Baroque Routes, the Rural Habitat Route, Architecture Without Frontiers, the Great Walser Road, the Venetian Villas, the Routes of the Celts, the Vikings Route, the Hanseatic World, the Lombards Route, the Mozart Itinerary, the Cistercian Routes, the Routes of Henry the Navigator, the Routes of Orthodox Monasticism, etc.

Each route has been equipped with its own logo whose use is recommended for information and safety.

Rural Habitat Route

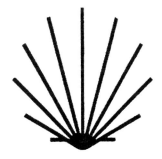

Roads to Santiago

The Roads to Santiago or Jacobean Roads were the first Pan - European itinerary. With reference to the original routes dating to the Middle Ages, this programme was launched in Santiago de Compostela (Spain) in 1987 with a predominantly religious dimension. Nowadays, they also take on a major cultural and tourism dimension that is not exclusive or oblivious to the former. A plan for tourism markers was undertaken in several countries (Spain, France, Portugal, Italy, Germany, and Belgium). The triptych showing the logo of the Roads to Santiago was issued in 5 European languages (Spanish, French, English, German and Italian). A manual for using the logo was published in Spanish.

Both UNESCO and WTO supported regional and inter-regional projects, such as Mundo Maya, the Silk Road or the Slave Route, each featuring a logo of its own, among other international routes[2].

MUNDO MAYA

Mundo Maya (The World of the Maya), called previously Ruta Maya, is a project launched with the participation of WTO and UNESCO in 1991 between five Central American countries: Guatemala, Honduras, El Salvador, Belize and the south of Mexico (States of Tabasco, Chiapas, Campeche, Yucatán and Quintana Roo).

THE SILK ROAD

UNESCO, together with WTO, launched the project entitled "Integrated study of the Silk Roads" by setting up a working group which, during the meeting held in Como (Italy), 13-15 October 1988, proposed that the UNESCO Cultural Cooperation Council should have a structure to promote the signposting of itineraries by establishing links between them. The logotype for these activities is an interlaced figure. The following countries have adopted this logo:

- Japan
- Republic of Korea
- China
- Kazakhstan
- Kyrgyzstan
- Pakistan
- Tadzhikistan
- Uzbekistan
- Turkmenistan
- Iran
- Turkey
- Azerbaijan
- Georgia
- Greece
- Egypt

The aim is to promote tourism along the historic route which became a real link between the East and West around 100 BC and lasted until the 15th century when newly discovered sea routes to Asia opened up. For 12.000 kilometers, the world's main commercial artery provided a link between some of the greatest civilizations the world has ever seen – the Chinese, Mongolian, Indian, Persianm Roman, Greek, Byzantine, Mesopotamina and Egyptian.

THE SLAVE ROUTE

"The Slave Route" is a scientific and cultural project of an international nature. It was developed by WTO and UNESCO and has its own logo. At a meeting held on 3 and 4 April 1995 in Accra under the auspices of WTO and UNESCO and in the spirit of the International Year of Tolerance, the participating countries expressed their wish to foster economic and human development and to rehabilitate, restore and promote the tangible and intangible heritage handed down by the slave trade for the purposes of cultural tourism, thereby emphasize the common nature of the slave trade between Africa, Europe, the Americas and the Caribbean.

The Accra Declaration, which was adopted on 29 April 1995 in Durban (South Africa) by the WTO Commission for Africa during its twenty-seventh meeting, led to a programme of work including an inventory, evaluation and appraisal of the sites, monuments and records in the territories, the preparation and joint implementation of strategies and programmes aiming to promote both international and national tourism and the adoption and application of measures that will promote the removal of barriers which hinder travel and tourist flows.

The very first activity carried out under the project was in relation to signs. It involved creating an identity for "The Slave Route" by means of a logo which is to be used by the partners in all communications and a promotional supporting document presenting the project that gives a description of the content and the agreement as well as a practical guide and a graphic chart. The logo is metaphorical - "a musical slave travelling through time and space, from the tom-tom to the saxophone".

3. TOURISM DESTINATION LOGOTYPES

A number of countries and tourism destinations, in particular through their national tourist offices which are responsible for the overall tourism promotion at home and abroad, have adopted an official logo (often incorporating a corresponding theme) in order to draw attention to their attractions and cultural and linguistic aspects.

As a rule, the official tourism logo is created after a careful study of the tourism resources and attractions in question.

Promotion logotypes (or logos) have come to be considered the tourist emblems of a country or a tourism destination. They can also act as an indication of belonging to the tourism sector of the country.

The application of the international law to the national tourism logos

The Paris Convention for the Protection of Industrial Property dated 20 March 1883 as revised in Stockholm on 14 July 1967 applies directly to NTA / NTO logotypes under the chapter *"Trade marks: prohibition for State emblems, official control signs and emblems of intergovernmental organizations"*. The Convention stipulates in its article 6c.:

"(a) The countries of the Union[3] agree to reject or invalidate registration and to prohibit by appropriate measures the use without proper authorization, either as a trade mark or as an element of such marks, coats of arms, flags and other emblems of State of countries of the Union, signs and official hallmarks for control and guarantee adopted by them as well as any imitation from the point of view of heraldry."

"(b) The above provisions also apply to coats of arms, flags and other emblems, initials or designations of inter-governmental international organizations of which one or more countries of the Union are members, with the exception of coats of arms, flags and other emblems, initials or designations which have already been covered by current international agreements for their protection."

Disciplines governing the use of national tourism logos

In most countries and destinations, the following bodies are entitled to use the national tourism promotion logo:

- national, regional and local tourism authorities
- any other public or official body in agreement with the logo holder (or without such authorization)
- commercial enterprises with authorization4.

Review of some NTO or NTA logos

Countries and destinations have developed logos in relation to their marketing strategy. These logos may change with the reformulation of the tourism image of the country or destination.

TOURISM VISUAL IDENTITY OF ARGENTINA

The National Secretariat for Tourism of Argentina developed in the nineties a new slogan "Argentina, the country of the six continents", and a logotype representing a symbolized Andean condor. The description of the logo (colours: Pantone 207C, Pantone 1665C and Pantone 289C, screens, corporate typography: Garamond, minimal sizes, official application for provinces), the basic conditions for its use (official application for provinces) and the signposting instructions (panels, bands, trade marks, etc.) were given in a published manual. Any use and variation in the conditions applied by the Secretariat must be approved by the latter, especially with respect to any promotional material, hotel advertisement or travel agency advertisement.

PORTUGAL'S IDENTITY MANUAL

Portugal's Identity Manual was published and circulated in 1992 to launch the new tourism logotype. It gives details on the graphics, colours, printing and inks to be used, recommendations for reproducing the logotype and indications for its protection.

THE SPANISH LOGO

This logotype, with the word ESPAÑA beneath the graphic illustration, suggests a sun in 4 colours • yellow, red, green and black. The brochure gives details on the standard colours (Europa Skala) with the colour percentages and linear design of the logotype with proportions. It indicates that the logotype is the property of the General Secretariat for Tourism and that it is managed and exploited by the independent organization TURESPAÑA. The latter must give express permission for its use by private persons or entities that must make an application in accordance with the Regulation of 22 April 1986 (Official State Bulletin dated 7 May 1986).

4. TRADEMARKS IN TOURISM

Trademarks in tourism are usually represented graphically by signs and symbols. They have very specific economic and legal aspects to be considered.

Basic elements

Trademarks pertain to the field of intellectual property rights. The critical aspects of using trademarks have been accentuated due to the ongoing liberalization of world trade. As much as in other sectors, trademarks are increasingly used in the tourism sector to make the company and its product distinct from other companies and thus compete for individual and corporate consumers. Apart from legal aspects, it is important that they are designed and depicted in much a way so as not to confuse and discomfort the traveller.

Trademarks have a different value to tourism symbols or signs. They go beyond the image of the logotype they bear to represent companies and organizations with a history and a culture. Over one million trademarks are registered annually in the world, and these figures are rising sharply in growing sectors such as tourism. A time gap is needed before a trade mark can be recognized nationally or internationally. When they begin to be successful, they become reference trademarks, either for the products or services they represent or for their inherent quality which leads them to represent values that amount to a sort of contract for loyalty or trust with their customers.

Regulated and legitimate use of trademarks contributes to transparency and respect for business ethics and helps to prevent confusion for consumers as well as commercial disputes.

Conventions on trademarks

International conventions exist and are applied for the protection of national trademarks in foreign countries, namely:

- *The Paris Convention for the Protection of Industrial Property dated 20 March 1883 (revised in 1967),*

- *The Madrid Agreement for the International Registration of Trademarks dated 14 April 1891,*

- *The Nice Agreement on International Classification of Products and Services for the purpose of registration of trade marks dated 15 February 1957,*

- *The Trade Related Agreement on Commercial Aspects of Intellectual Property Rights of the World Trade Organization dated 15 April 1994 (TRIPS).*

The TRIPS agreement, which came into force on 1 January 1995, provides that *"any sign, or combination of signs, serving to distinguish the products or services of one enterprise from those of other enterprises may constitute a trade mark. Such signs, especially words, including the names of persons, letters, figures, figurative elements and combinations of colours as well as any combination of such signs, may be registered as trade marks".* (Article 15, section 2: Trademarks).

The agreement also states that the parties to it *"shall publish each trademark either before registration or as soon as possible after registration, and shall arrange for a reasonable possibility of having the registration cancelled".*

Article 16, line 1 covers conferred rights: *"The owner of a registered trademark shall have the exclusive right of preventing any third parties acting without consent from using in commercial operations identical or similar signs for identical or similar products or services to those for which the trademark was registered in cases where such usage would lead to confusion. In the case of usage of an identical sign for identical products or services, the risk of confusion is presumed to exist. The above rights shall not affect any previously existing right..."*

Paragraph 2 confirms that article 6b of the Paris Convention (1967) *"Trademarks: well-known trademarks", that is, the Paris Convention for the protection of industrial property of 20 March 1893 as revised in Stockholm on 14 July 1967, shall apply, mutatis mutandis, to services. In order to determine if a trade mark is well-known, the parties to the Agreements shall take into account the fame of the trademark amongst the concerned part of the public, including the fame in the country concerned as a result of promotion of the trademark".*

The same article will also apply, mutatis mutandis, to products or services which are not similar to those for which a trade mark has been registered, provided that use of the trademark for these products or services indicates a link between these products or services and the owner of the registered trademark and on the condition that this use might harm the interests of the holder of the registered trademark. This means that all tourism products and services are affected by the TRIPS agreement and that tourism enterprises must conform to the provisions of the 1994 Agreement.

The agreement also protects geographic indications serving to identify a product or a service as having originated in the territory of a party to the Agreement. This issue is very important in the area of travel and tourism.

The TRIPS agreement covers "Control of anti-competitive practices in contract licenses" (Section 8, article 40) which are very frequent in the tourism sector. The design of trademarks falls under intellectual property which the TRIPS Agreement also aims to protect by requesting the countries that are party to the Agreement to include in their legislation procedures enforcing compliance with industrial property rights, as well as rapid corrective measures to prevent any violation of these and corrective measures constituting a means of dissuasion against any subsequent violation.

With respect to the prevention and resolution of disputes (Part V, Articles 63 and 64), the agreement requires that there should be transparency in laws, regulations and final judicial and administrative decisions with a view to facilitating the exchange of information.

Role of NTAs and NTOs

NTAs and NTOs begun to take interest in regulations for the registration and protection of trademarks only a few years ago. In general, they make recommendations on this matter or when asked for advice.

Disputes on registered trademarks may be resolved by means of arbitration or through their commercial courts. In a few cases, there are special procedures for disputes in the area of tourism.

EXAMPLES

National administrations and organs responsible for tourism trade-marks in the different regions of the world: some examples

Africa

Malawi: Control of tourism trademarks under the authority
               of the Ministry of Trade and Industry

Morocco: Control under the authority of the Ministry of Finance,
               Department of Taxes and Registration
               (NTA is responsible for quality control)

Americas

Argentina: Trademark registration and intellectual property rights
               are considered on a national level

Aruba: Control exercised by the Chamber of Commerce

Bolivia: General Department of the National Office
               for Industrial Property

México: Mexican Institute for Industrial Property

Peru   Institute for Fair Trading Practices and Intellectual
               Property

South Asia/Asia and the Pacific

China: Administration for Industry and Trade

Maldives: Ministry of Trade, Industry and Labour

Sri Lanka: Register of Public and Private Enterprises

Europe

Cyprus:	Register of Official Enterprises and Emblems
Finland:	National Office of Licenses and Registration
Israel:	Ministry of Justice
Slovakia:	Office for Industrial Property of the Slovak Republic
Former Yugoslav Republic of Macedonia (FYROM):	the Office for the Protection of Industrial Property
Turkey:	Turkish Institute for Standardization

Middle East

Iraq:	Ministry of Trade
Jordan:	Ministry of Trade, Industry and Supplies

Tourism signs for Lisbon Expo'98

In 1996, a study on the standardization of tourism symbols was published by the Planning and Study Office of the General Directorate for Tourism of Portugal which provided an index of tourism signs and symbols in the following areas:

- culture
- leisure
- nature
- infrastructure
- transport and travel
- tourist facilities
- business tourism
- health
- events

It was a very useful tool for the world exposition, LISBON EXPO'98.

5. SPECIAL EVENTS

Logotypes for special events of importance for tourism such as tourism and other fairs, exhibitions, celebrations (e.g. special days), cultural festivals, sports, games, races, world expositions, etc. are needed to carry and transmit their graphical image, which can be used as effective information, advertising and marketing tools.

It is worth-mentioning that not all major events, even if they are periodically organized at regular intervals (e.g. World Tourism Day held every 27 September), have their own logotypes. Those responsible for such events may equally conclude that the use of a logo is not cost-effective, or that another new logo may not be noticed among the many logos already existing, or, on the contrary, that the adoption of a logo may help carry the message and better achieve the objective, be it awareness-raising, participation or even sale. This should be examined on a case by case basis.

6. QUALITY LABELS

Tourism quality marks or labels represent an effort intended to convey a message of excellence or compliance with determined quality standards to individual and corporate customers. They can be found in travel literature and in establishments and equipment. They can be used by establishments which have been awarded the distinction concerned by the competent and recognized body in the field (a national body or a professional organization[5] and may also take the form of a recommendation. Some of the symbols may have a more concrete meaning to professional bodies (e.g. tour operators contracting hotels), others are aimed at the public at large.

As quality-related labels are a very recent development, their promotional, commercial and informational effectiveness will be checked over time. In the meantime, it is important to know the meaning of specific distinctions or labels.

ISO Certification

The respective labels (e.g. (ISO 9001, ISO 9002, ISO 9004-2, ISO 14000) found in some tourist establishments, in particular hotels, or in travel literature, inform about the compliance with ISO standards, such as procedures used in management (organization, written procedures, control of key documents, keeping registers, carrying out periodical checks, identifying and correcting errors, improving communication...) which have been certified by a competent third party. Compliance with ISO standards does not guarantee quality, but implies such expectation by having created a favourable management environment for quality at the establishment concerned. The system is international and primarily of interest to tourism companies within tourism distribution channels (e.g. to tour operators with respect to certified hotels).

Regional symbols

European Ecology Label (eco-label)

Established by regulation CE 880/92, this distinction, alongside ISO 14000, is useful for tourism establishments interested in sound environmental management.

National quality symbols

Recent examples come from Spain and Switzerland.

Spain

Started as a quality mark for hotels and tourist apartments known as ICHE (designed by the Instituto para la Calidad Hotelera Española/Institute for Spanish Hotel Quality), its application has been extended, at the present stage (year 2000), to travel agencies, restaurants, campsites, ski and mountain stations and rural tourism establishments, to be managed by the sole Institute for Spanish Tourism Quality (ICTE). The concession of the quality mark is based on the following principles:

- its voluntary and self-regulatory character,
- a neutral and rigorous system of standards design and certification,
- the existence of a Certification Committee formed by prestigious and responsible personalities and institutions not related to the sub-sector concerned.

Switzerland

Initiated and agreed to by a wide spectrum of tourism related bodies: NTO - Tourisme Suisse, the Swiss Tourism Union, GastroSuisse, the Swiss Hotel Association, the Swiss Union of Cable Railways (ASC), the Swiss Union of Public Transport (UTP), the Conference of

Regional Directors (RDK), the Association of Swiss Directors of Tourism (ASDT, this voluntary and horizontal system has from the outset been applied to hotels, holiday flats, campsites, restaurants, tourist information offices, mountain railways, water transport, sport centres, etc.

Three stages of quality standards are designated by corresponding quality marks:

1. Applies to establishments which have created the basis for the development of quality service.
2. Applies to establishments which have instituted management for quality to back quality service.

3. Applies to establishments which boast having the system of total quality management (TQM)

Classification symbols

Graphic symbols used for tourism establishment classification purposes, by means of stars, crowns, keys, forks, shells, etc., primarily carry the message of the establishment physical characteristics, such as space, size, the type and number of items featured, as well as the price level. Such characteristics also give rise to quality expectations, these, however, cannot be satisfied on the basis of classification alone since quality can be ensured in all establishment categories (and vice versa).

The Themis/OMT TEDQUAL Certification Logo

This logo reflects the certification for quality and efficiency in the tourism education programmes of a teaching institution. WTO has developed, through its Themis Foundation, the TEDQUAL Certification System (Tourism Education Quality), with the aim of contributing to competitiveness in tourism education, by proposing a methodology and voluntary standards with a universal scope to foster the qualitative definition of tourism education systems. TEDQUAL is thus a quality assurance system in tourism education and training, to which all those teaching institutions and corporations, whether public or private, who wish to certify specific Tourism Education Programmes (TEPs) can voluntarily subscribe.

[1] Source: Asociaci which all those teaching institutions and corporations, whether public or private, who wish to certify specific Tourism

[2] Examples of other important international cultural and tourist routes are given below (according to the WTO survey):
Argentina: Route of the Incas, Route of the Jesuit Missions
Mexico: Colonial Cities, Barrancas del Cobre, the Cortés Route
Finland: Route of the Nordic Kings
Israel: Spice Road (under negotiation)
Italy: The 'consular roads' of Roman origin starting in Rome, such as the Via Aurelia leading to France and Spain, and the Via Romea, originating in the area of Ravenna included in the European itinerary E45 going from Sicily all the way up to Denmark) of which some remains are still visible in Germany. The ancient Via Francegina crosses Tuscany, the north of Italy and the Alps and leads to France National Road 12 from Abetone and Brennero originates in Tuscany and leads to Austria across the Brenner pass.
Czech Republic: Burgenstrasse
Slovakia: International Danube Cycloroute

[3] i.e. the assembly of parties to the Convention.

[4] According to the WTO survey, only one country reported to accept the use of the national tourism promotion logo by commercial enterprises without permission (the Former Yugoslav Republic of Macedonia (FYROM)).

[5] e.g. ,the Automobile Association of America, Michelin in France (applicable to establishments in and outside France), etc.

ANNEXES

ANNEX 1

SYMBOLS LISTED IN THE WTO REPORT ON THE STANDARDIZATION OF TOURIST SIGNS AND SYMBOLS (1989)

In 1989, WTO produced an informative document entitled ìReport on the Standardization of Tourist Signs and Symbolsì (PG(VI)B.5.1) which basically dealt with tourist attractions.

The aim of this activity was *"to take stock of the situation as regards the use of signs and symbols (other than signs for identifying tourism plant and facilities) to indicate natural, cultural and historical attractions of interest to the tourist. As it is, in a certain number of countries signs and symbols have long been in use not only to indicate tourist attractions but also tourism services and facilities..."*
The report suggests:

- to facilitate the selection of tourist sites which could be designated using standardized signs and symbols;

- to establish universally recognizable pictograms which could be used for signposting these tourist attractions.

The report shows that various concepts have been used to denote the same attraction or activity, as for example:

ATTRACTION OR ACTIVITY	REPRESENTED BY
Park	Fence; trees, tree with picnic table
Panorama	Camera; sunset; telescope; man on a mountain looking at the view
Cave	Entrance to cave with person in it; Entrance without person
Waterfall	Mountain with waterfall;

Waterfall alone	
Volcano	
Mountain	
Fauna/wildlife	
Bird; deer	
Religious monuments	Various structures with religious symbol
Historical monuments	Obelisk; arch; classic structure
Ruins	Broken arch; broken pottery; cave paintings

A good sample of symbols (pictograms) was received from the countries and territories that replied to the WTO survey. As a result, it was possible to present an indicative list of tourist attractions as follows:

NATURE
Parks
Vista
Natural phenomena
Beaches
Gardens
Bird-watching
Flora and Fauna
Scenic routes

STRUCTURES AND MONUMENTS
Archaeological sites
Historical (castles, forts, walled towns)
Modern architecture
Religious (convents, churches, synagogues, temples)
Landmarks (lighthouses, towers, dwellings)

RECREATION & SPORTS
Physical fitness
Water sports
Snow sports
Horse riding
Mountain sports
Hiking (routes)

Hunting
Fishing
Amusement parks
Tennis/squash
Golf
Cycling routes
Sports events
Race tracks
Camping
Surfing
Boating

TRANSPORT
Old train rides
Boat trips
Ballooning
Carriages
Cable cars

CULTURE
Museums
Art galleries
Musical events
Drama
Cinema
Poetry readings
Exhibitions
Dance
Collections (miniatures, tapestries, etc.)

GASTRONOMICAL
Typical of region or country
Cooking courses
Elaboration of products (visits to vineyards, plants)
Food festivals

COMMERCIAL
Shopping
Specialty shops
Workshops/factories
Markets

ENTERTAINMENT
Folklore
Night-clubs
Festivals (jazz, music)
Special events
Theme park (water, historical)
Shows

HANDICRAFTS
Crafts shows
Workshops
Exhibitions
Ceramics
Woodwork
Metal works

EDUCATIONAL
Courses Seminars (crafts, cooking, dance, language, nature)

ANNEX 2

THE VIENNA CONVENTION ON ROAD SIGNS AND SIGNALS (1968)

The Convention on road signs and signals is the first main tool dealing with standardization of signs and symbols for road traffic. The Convention was adopted during the United Nations Conference on Road Traffic, held in Vienna (7 October-8 November 1968) and entered into force on 6 June 1978.

This Convention was ratified by the following 59 countries (until January 1996):

Austria, Bahrain, Belarus, Belgium, Bosnia and Herzegovina, Brazil, Bulgaria, Central African Republic, Chile, China, Costa Rica, Cote d'Ivoire, Croatia, Cuba, Czech Republic, Denmark, Ecuador, Estonia, Finland, France, Germany, Ghana, Greece, Holy See, Hungary, India, Indonesia, Iran, Iraq, Italy, Kazakhstan, Kuwait, Latvia, Lithuania, Luxembourg, Mexico, Morocco, Norway, Pakistan, Philippines, Poland, Portugal, Republic of Korea, Romania, Russian Federation, San Marino, Senegal, Seychelles, Slovakia, Spain, Sweden, Switzerland, Tajikistan, Thailand, Ukraine, United Kingdom, Venezuela, Yugoslavia, Zaire (Republic of Congo).

The contracting parties recognize in this convention "that international uniformity of road signs, signals and symbols and of road markings is necessary in order to facilitate international road traffic and to increase safety".

The Convention agreed on the establishment of 113 standardized road signs, classified in the following categories:

1. **Danger Warning Signs**, intended to warn road-users of a danger on the road and to inform them of its nature;

2. **Regulatory signs**, intended to inform road-users of special obliga-

tions, restrictions or prohibitions with which they must comply; they are sub-divided into:

(i)   Priority signs,
(ii)   Prohibitory or restrictive signs; and
(iii)   Mandatory signs;

3. **Informative signs,** intended to guide road-users while they are travelling or to provide them with other information which may be useful; they are sub-divided into:

(i)   Advanced signs
(ii)   Direction signs
(iii)   Road identification signs
(iv)   Place identification signs
(v)   Confirmatory signs
(vi)   Other signs providing useful information for drivers of vehicles
(vii)   Other signs indicating facilities which may be useful for road-users.

Annexes to the Convention

From the eight Annexes to the Convention, seven present models for signs and Annex 8 deals with road markings.

Annex 1
Danger warning signs, other than those placed at approaches to intersections or level crossing

Section A.
Models for danger warning signs
The convention defines the danger warning signs which shall be an equilateral triangle having one side horizontal and the opposite vertex above it; the ground is white or yellow and the border red. The side of the normal sized sign of model A shall measure approximately 0.90 m; the small sized sign shall measure not less than 0.60 m.

Section B.

Symbols for danger warning and instructions for the use of such signs

* Dangerous bend or bends (left, right, double bend, or succession of more than two bends, etc.):
  Dangerous descent
  Steep ascent
  Carriage narrows
  Swing bridge
  Road leads on to quay or river bank
  Uneven road
  Slippery road
  Loose gravel
  Falling rocks
  Pedestrian crossing
  Children
  Cyclists entering or crossing
  Cattle or other animals crossing
  Road works
  Light signals
  Airfield
  Cross-wind
  Two-way traffic

* Other dangers (in particular to give warning of intersections with railway tracks at which rail traffic proceeds very slowly and road traffic is regulated by a railway - man)

Annex 2

Signs regulating priority at intersections, danger warning signs at approaches to intersections and signs regulating priority on narrow sections of road

Section A.

Signs regulating priority at intersections

"give away" sign
"stop" sign
"priority road" sign

"end of priority" sign

Section B.
Danger warning signs at approaches to intersections

The symbols shall be black or dark blue

Intersection where the priority is that prescribed by the general priority rule in force in the country
Intersection with a road the users of which must give away (priority)
Intersection with a road to whose users drivers must give way
Roundabout

Section C.
Signs regulating priority on narrow sections of road

Sign indicating priority for incoming traffic
Sign indicating priority over oncoming traffic

Annex 3
Signs concerning level-crossings

Section A.
Danger warning systems

Section B.
Signs to be placed in the immediate vicinity of level-crossings

Annex 4:
Regulatory signs other than priority, standing and parking signs

Section A.
Prohibitory or restrictive signs

Shape and size
Prohibitory and restrictive signs shall be circular; their diameter shall be not less than 0.60 m outside built-up areas and not less than 0.40 m

in built-up areas

Prohibition and restriction of entry
• No entry for any power driven vehicle except two-wheeled motor cycles without side-car
• No entry for motor cycles
• No entry for mopeds
• No entry for goods vehicles
• No entry for any power driven vehicle drawing a trailer other than a semi-trailer or a single axle trailer
• No entry for pedestrians
• No entry for animal ñdrawn vehicles
• No entry for handcarts
• No entry for power driven agricultural vehicles
• No entry for vehicles having an over-all width exceeding ... meters
• No entry for vehicles having an over-all height exceeding ... meters
• No entry for vehicles exceeding... tons laden weight
• No entry for vehicles having a weight exceeding .. tons on one axle
• No entry for vehicles or combinations of vehicles exceeding ... meters in length
• Prohibition of turning
• Prohibition of U-turns
• Prohibition of overtaking
• Speed limit
• Prohibition of the use of audible warning devices
• Prohibition of passing without stopping
• End of prohibition or restriction

Section B.
Mandatory signs

Shape and size
Mandatory signs shall be circular; their diameter shall be not less than 0.60 m outside built-up areas and not less than 0.40 m inside built-up areas. However, signs having a diameter of not less than 0.30 m may be used in conjunction with traffic light signals or on traffic islands.

Colour
The signs shall be blue and the symbols shall be white or of a light

colour, or, alternatively, the signs shall be white with a red rim and the symbols shall be black.

Description of the signs
Direction to be followed
Pass this side
Compulsory roundabout
Compulsory cycle track
Compulsory foot-path
Compulsory track for riders on horseback
Compulsory minimum speed
End of compulsory minimum speed
Snow chains compulsory

Annex 5
Informative signs other than parking signs

Shape and size
Informative signs shall be rectangular; however, direction signs may be in the shape of an elongated rectangle with the longer side horizontal, terminated in an arrowhead.

Colour
Informative signs shall bear either white or light-coloured symbols or inscriptions on a dark ground, or dark-coloured symbols or inscriptions on a white or light-colored ground.

Section A.
Advance direction signs

Advance signs such as for no through road

Section B.
Direction signs

Section C.
Place identification signs

Section D.
Confirmatory signs

Section E.
Pedestrian crossing
Section F.
Other signs providing useful information for drivers of vehicles

- Hospital sign
- One-way road sign
- No through road sign
- Signs notifying an entry to or exit from a motorway
- Signs notifying an entry to or exit from a road on which the traffic rules are the same as on a motorway
- Signs notifying a bus or tramway stop
- Road open or closed sign

Section G.
Signs giving notice of facilities which may be useful to road users

Shape and colour
These signs shall have a blue or green ground; they shall bear a white or yellow rectangle on which the symbol hall be displayed. On the blue or green band at the bottom of the sign, the distance to the facility indicated, or to the entry to the road leading to it, may be inscribed in white.

Description of symbols
First aid symbols
Breakdown service (rest area)
Telephone
Filling station
Hotel or Motel
Restaurant
Refreshments or Cafeteria
Picnic site
Starting-point for walk
Camping site
Caravan site

Camping and caravan site
Youth hostel

Annex 6
Standing and parking signs

Section A.
Signs prohibiting or restricting standing or parking

<u>Shape and colour</u>
These signs shall be circular; their diameter shall not be less than 0.60 m outside built-up areas and not less than 0.25 m in built-up areas. The ground shall be blue and the border and oblique bars red.

<u>Description of signs</u>
Parking prohibited
Standing and parking prohibited
Alternate parking
Limited duration parking zone

Section B.
Signs providing useful information on parking

• The "Parking" sign
• Sign indicating the exit from a limited duration parking zone

Annex 7
Additional panels

These panels shall have either a white or yellow ground and a black, dark blue or red rim, in which case the distance or length shall be inscribed in black or dark blue; or a black or dark blue ground and a white, yellow or red rim, in which case the distance or length shall be inscribed in white or yellow

Annex 8
Road markings

Road surface markings
They should be of non-skid materials and should not protrude more than 6 mm above the level of the carriageway. Studs or similar devices used for marking should not protrude more than 1.5 cm above the level of the carriageway.

Longitudinal markings
Their dimensions are defined in the Annex, in particular the traffic lane markings.

Marking for particular situations
Such as the use of continuous lines, the border lines indicating the limits of the carriage way, the marking of obstructions and the guide lines for turning vehicles.

Transverse markings
They shall be wider than longitudinal markings because of the angle at which the driver sees markings on the carriage ways.

Stop lines

Lines indicating points at which drivers must give way

Pedestrian crossings

Cyclist crossing

Arrow markings

Oblique parallel lines

Word markings such as stop, bus, taxi.

Standing and parking regulations

Markings on the carriageway and on adjacent structures

ANNEX 3

INTERNATIONAL SIGNS TO PROVIDE GUIDANCE TO PERSONS AT AIRPORTS AND MARINE TERMINALS

A joint ICAO-IMO publication (1995 - doc 9430)

The contents of this publication reflect the process used in preparing this document. It therefore consists of a general section explaining the principles concerning the use of signs, a section depicting signs which may be common to both marine and air terminals, and two other sections specific to either airports or marine terminals, all covering 42 referents.

SECTION I.
GENERAL PRINCIPLES CONCERNING THE USE OF SIGNS

The main concepts are the following:

Number of signs

"The number of signs used at airports and marine terminals should be kept to minimum consistent with the need to provide guidance to air and sea travellers and the general public"

Location and size

"Where appropriate, signs should indicate both the direction to and the location of the facilities in question. The signs should be installed in conspicuous places and should not be obscured by obstructions or have to compete for attention with advertising or other signs. The sign-carrier should be moderately contrasted to its environment (i.e. a lighter environment requires a darker sign-carrier surface, a darker environment requires a lighter surface).

The signs should be large enough to be recognized at reasonable distances and, where necessary, should be internally or externally illuminated. Within each terminal building, the relationship of the size of the symbols to the sign as a whole should be the same on all signs.

Directional signs should be rectangular and location signs should be either square or rectangular...

When a sign symbol having implicit or explicit directional characteristics, such as bus or Helicopter, is combined with a directional arrow, it should be laterally reversed, if necessary, so as to point in the same direction as the arrow, thereby avoiding directional ambiguity."

The use of words

"As far as possible, symbols alone should be used without words.

Letters and figures

"Where words are considering necessary, a simple typeface should be used and should be standardized on all signs throughout the terminal building and, if possible, at all terminal buildings at airports and marine terminals in the same country.

...

The colour co-ordination of lettering and background should be left to the national or local authority. In general dark lettering on light background is more legible because of the optimum brightness contrast..."

Colours

"The same colour scheme should be used on all signs in the airport or marine terminal building and, if possible, in all terminal buildings at airports and marine terminals in the same country.

SECTION II.
INTERNATIONAL SIGNS TO PROVIDE GUIDANCE TO PERSONS AT AIRPORTS AND MARINE TERMINALS

1.   BAGGAGE CLAIM AREA
2.   BAGGAGE CART/TROLLEY
3.   BAGGAGE LOCKERS

4. BAGGAGE STORAGE
5. INFORMATION
6. BUS
7. TRAIN
8. TAXI
9. CAR HIRE
10. TOILETS (GENERAL)
11. TOILETS (MEN)
12. TOILETS (WOMEN)
13. TELEPHONE
14. POSTAL FACILITY
15. TELEGRAMS/CABLES/TELEX
16. BANK OR CURRENCY EXCHANGE OFFICE
17. BAR
18. RESTAURANT
19. COFFEE SHOP (OR EQUIVALENT FACILITY)
20. DRINKING WATER
21. SHOPPING AREA
22. FIST AID [1]
23. PHARMACY [1]
24. LOST AND FOUND
25. NURSERY
26. ACESS FOR DISABLED PERSONS
27. ELEVATORS
28. HOTEL RESERVATIONS
29. NO SMOKING
30. NO ENTRY/NO TRESPASSING
31. CARRY NO WEAPONS ON BOARD
32. DIRECTIONAL ARROWS
33. ENLARGED DESIGN OF DIRECTIONAL ARROW

[1] International signs to provide guidance to persons at airports and marine terminals, ICAO, IMO, London 1995, IMO sales number: IMO-370M / ICAO sales number: Doc 9636-C/1114. The document explains that if in a sign there is a cross, in countries where the cross is not a recognized emblem, another appropriate emblem may be used instead.

SECTION III.
INTERNATIONAL SIGNS TO PROVIDE GUIDANCE TO PERSONS AT AIRPORTS

34.   ARRIVALS
35.   DEPARTURES
36.   CONNECTING FLIGHTS
37.   HELICOPTER

SECTION IV.
INTERNATIONAL SIGNS TO PROVIDE GUIDANCE TO PERSONS AT MARINE TERMINALS

38.   ARRIVAL
39.   DEPARTURE
40.   FOOT PASSENGERS
41.   CARS
42.   LORRIES

ANNEX 4

NUMERICAL INDEX AND SURVEY OF THE
PUBLIC INFORMATION SYMBOLS ADOPTED IN ISO 7001

001	Direction
002	Smoking allowed
003	Helicopter
004	Tram streetcar
005	Bus
006	Male/Man
007	Female
008	Telephone
009	Gasoline Station
010	Drinking water (on tap)
011	Stairs
012	Taxi
013	Waiting room
014	Fire Extinguisher
015	Toilet
016	Toilet for men
017	Toilet for women
018	Rubbish receptacle
019	No rubbish
020	Currency exchange
021	Elevator/Lift
022	Aircraft
023	Parking for a specified type of vehicle
024	Boat
025	Nature reserve
026	Way in
027	Way out
028	Left luggage
029	Sporting activities
030	Accommodation
031	Restaurant
032	Hospital

033	Cable car, large capacity
034	Cable car, small capacity
035	Cable railway/ratchet railway
036	Chair lift
037	Close overhead safety bar
038	Open overhead safety bar
039	Close safety bar
040	Open safety bar
041	Line up two by two
042	Line up three by three
043	Raise ski tips
044	Ski lift
045	Bath
046	Shower
047	Tennis
048	Squash/ racket Ball
049	Lost property/Lost and found
050	Tickets
051	Double Chairlift
052	Triple Chairlift
053	Quadruple Chairlift
054	Line up four by four
055	Foot passengers have to get off
056	Skiers have to get off
057	Steep-slope ski lift

ANNEX 5

INDEX OF SIGNS AND SYMBOLS USED AS VARIANTS TO DENOTE THE EXISTENCE AND STATUS OF EQUIPMENT, FACILITIES AND SERVICES FOR PEOPLE WITH DISABILITIES

For the purpose of this publication the term people with disabilities includes all persons who, owing to the environment being encountered, have special needs while travelling, particularly individuals with physical, sensory and mental disabilities; other medical conditions requiring special care; elderly persons, and others in need of temporary assistance (WTO, Annex to resolution A/RES/284(IX) of the General Assembly at its ninth session (Buenos Aires — Argentina, 30 September - 4 October 1991).

If there are only a few specific symbols directly linked with disabilities and internationally recommended for standardization, many variants (alternative symbol or two and more joint symbols) may exist to denote the existence and status of public and visitor equipment, tourist facilities and services for persons with disabilities.

In some cases, the use of symbols can be linked with a level of accessibility, as defined, for example, by the European Union Tourism for All Accessible Accommodation Standard [1]/[2].

1. General public and visitor information

The international symbol of access for the disabled[3]

Adopted in 1969 by Rehabilitation International (RI), a union of national and international organizations working for persons with disabilities in about 60 countries.

The RI symbol, according to ISO (ISO/145, London 1976) has the following advantages:

- it is outstanding and expressive

- it is simple but has yet an aesthetic form
- it is easily identifiable both at a short and a long distance
- it cannot be mixed up with any other symbol
- it is easily remembered
- it is easy to reproduce and to manufacture in all sizes, materials and colours.

1.1. Variant - accessible to a wheelchair user travelling independently

2. Access with assistance

2.1. Variant - accessible to a wheelchair user with assistance

3. Access to someone with limited mobility but able to walk a few paces and up to a maximum of three steps

4. Access for persons with walking aids

5. Facilities for visually impaired people

6. Facilities for persons with hearing impairments

7. Parking with variants for user with assistance and people with limited mobility

8. Ramps (< 5% and width of 0,9 m)

9. Mobile lifts

10. Stairs with access to wheelchair user

11. Accessible lift (1m length ñ 0,8 m width)

12. Obstacles

13. Thresholds accessible to wheelchair user

14. Toilets accessible to wheelchair user (door opening outside and minimum of 1,9 m length ñ 0,9 m width) (Unisex)

14.1 Toilets idem (Men)

14.2 Toilets idem (Women)

15. Guide dogs welcome

16. Information in Braille

17. Special wireless guide system for persons with vision impairments

18. Public telephone with access to wheelchair user and people with short stature (low situation)
19. Repair and replacement facilities for prostheses and equipment
20. Pharmacy with access to wheelchair user or selling drugs and prostheses and equipment for persons with disabilities
21. Veterinary clinics for service animals
22. Supplier of specialized medical services
23. Staff trained to deal with person with disabilities
24. Shuttle services to and from rail, air, bus and marine terminals with access to wheelchair users.

2. Tourist equipment and facilities

25. Restaurant with access to wheelchair user
26. Bar with access to wheelchair user
27. Cafeteria with access to wheelchair user
28. Discotheque with access to wheelchair user
29. Garden with access to wheelchair user
30. Shop with access to wheelchair user
31. Roll-in showers
32. Alarm systems suitable for deaf and blind visitors
33. Doors of minimum width of 0,7 m
34. Accessible bedrooms with surface of the bed between 450mm & 540 mm above the floor
35. Television & video equipped for persons with disabilities
36. Room telephone with large keys
37. Room telephone with inductive couplers and amplifiers
38. Swimming pool with access to persons with disabilities
39. Fitness centre with access to persons with disabilities
40. Adequate seating for persons in wheelchairs in conference facilities

3. Accommodation facilities with possible certified levels of accessibility

1. Ramps (covering all areas outside and inside accommodation)
2. Thresholds (covering all areas outside and inside accommodation)

3. External and internal step approach (where there is no ramp there are to be no more than the specified steps, at any point, to the entrance)
4. Handrails (external and internal)
5. Main entrance doors (covering all areas outside and inside accommodation)
6. Internal doors (covering all areas outside and inside accommodation)
7. Door handles (covering all areas outside and inside accommodation)
8. Paths, passageways and corridors (all routes that disabled guest would use - covering all areas outside and inside accommodation)
9. Unobstructed space clear of door swing (covering entrance and reception areas, restaurant/dining room /bar, lounge, bedrooms and bathrooms, public accessible toilets, leisure and conference facilities)
10. Tables (covering restaurants, dining/meeting/banqueting rooms and bars and dressing table or a desk in accessible bedrooms)
11. Light switches, curtain pulls and hanging rail/robe hooks
12. Mirrors in all accessible public toilets, accessible bedrooms and ensuite bathrooms
13. Public entrance and interior general
14. Accessible public toilets
15. Lift
16. Conference, meeting and banqueting facilities
17. Leisure and sports facilities inside and outside
18. Accessible bedrooms
19. Bathroom
20. Bathroom where only a shower is available
21. Bathroom ensuite toilet

[1] For visually impaired people or blind, or (sometimes, as well as) in addition hard-of-hearing or deaf.
From the proposal of the European Union Tourism for All Accessible Accommodation Standard, European Forum With Disabilities, 1996, Source: WTO.

[2] CERTIFIED LEVELS OF ACCESSIBILITY
Physical Accessibility
Sensory Accessibility
Level 4. Total accessibility for all people
Inclusive
Level 3. Total accessibility in all areas for independent wheelchair users
Stand Alone
Level 2. Accessible in basic areas including independent wheelchair users
Stand Alone
Level 1. Accessible for people with ambulant Disability
Stand Alone
The symbol is added to a number (1,2,3 or 4). European Union Tourism for All Accessible Accommodation Standard, European Forum with Disabilities, 1996. These numbers are mainly used in tourist guides and brochures.
Graphic symbols quoted in bold type are reproduced in Chapter 3.

[3] The term "disabled" (suggesting that the person in question is not able) is currently challenged and proposed to be replaced by the term "persons with disabilities" in conformity with the position of the National Councils gathered at the European Forum of People with Disabilities (1996).

ANNEX 6

DESIGNING PRINT COMMUNICATIONS FOR
THE MATURE READER

(Excerpts from "Strategies for Targeting the Senior Market" by Hal Norvell, AARP in association with ITT Hartford, Second International Conference on Senior Tourism, 1996, WTO)

How to design
What can you do to design print and graphics that will "target" people 40 plus? How can you help assure that they will be able to read and give you the total attention you pay designers and printers for?

Type Size
Research suggests that text copy printed in type that is slightly larger than commonly used is effective for older readers. Most experts recommend that text be set in 11 to 14 point type. 12 point type is usually sufficient, depending on leading.

Leading, Page
Two points of leading - the space between lines of type - is most commonly used in text copy for readers of all ages. Using more than two points of leading can be counterproductive when using 14 point or larger type. Words appear to float on the page and will taker longer to read and understand.

Type Style
As the human eye ages, its ability to focus on near material decreases. The older reader will become more dependent on recognizing forms and letters by the crispness of their edges. Type styles with clean, crisp edges will help readers recognize and process the words.

Serif is Preferred
Serif is preferred for text copy. Ornate faces, such as italic, are not recommended because letters that appear cluttered and blurry are difficult to define. Upper-and-lower case is best. Type consisting of all capital letters makes the words hard to differentiate.

Design Format

For books and magazines 8.6"x11"or 20 cm x 30 cm, a two-column format works well. Each column should be roughly 3 " or 8.5 cm wide, with 3/8 " or 1 cm between columns. If you choose a one-column format, each line of copy should be between five and six inches wide or 12 cm and 15 cm wide.

Short, Crisp Paragraphs

Short, crisp paragraphs and sentences are easily digested by readers of any age. "White space" is helpful because it automatically organizes information into bite-size packages for processing.

Contrast 1

As a general rule, the greater the contrast on the page, the easier it is for the older reader to identify an image.

Contrast 2, The Retina Receives Less Light

As we age, the retina of the eye receives less light. Therefore, printed materials for the older reader should compensate for an increased sensitivity to glare and reduced sensitivity to contrast.

Contrast 3, Black and Dark Ink

Black and dark ink on white Matte paper is your best choice for printed material. Dark ink absorbs the light, while white paper reflects it.

Dark on Dark

Many design artists prefer colour on colour. For our eyes as we age, however, such subtlety becomes very difficult to read. In fact, the messages may disappear entirely.

Graded Contrast

The easiest design to read has the greatest contrast. Remember, however, that good design can include using the same colours or highly contrasting colours. The designer simply needs to work harder and more creatively.

Supporting Visuals, Colour 1

As we age, the lens of the eye begins to yellow. Colours will appear duller, especially in the blue-green end of the colour spectrum. The older reader will see less contrast between those colours. Reds, oranges, and yellows are relatively unaffected by ageing.

Supporting Visuals, Charts, 2
Graphs and charts should use colours with high contrast. High contrast is especially critical in bar graphs and maps. Always check your colour choices through a light yellow filter.

Supporting Visuals, 3
As we grow older, it takes us longer to recognize and process information. It also becomes more difficult to find information when it is embedded in a display.

Supporting Visuals, 4
For example, older readers have trouble seeing type placed over art. The type disappears into the art, and the reader will have more difficulty separating and extracting the information from other stimuli in the page.

ANNEX 7

WTO EXECUTIVE COUNCIL RECOMMENDATIONS ON
TOURISM SIGNS AND SYMBOLS
(adopted on 30 November 2000 by Executive Council decision
CE/DEC/6(LXIII-LXIV on the proposal of the WTO Quality Support Committee)

a. Recommendation on the tourist information sign

The Executive Council,

Recalling the revised text of recommendation B (13 bis) made to Governments by the Regional Commission for Tourism in Europe (RCTE) of the International Union of Official Travel Organizations/IUOTO (Amsterdam, Netherlands, 28 April 1975), that the sign to indicate the location of a tourist information office should conform to either of the two model signs shown in appendix 1 to this recommendation;

Considering the current common use of this sign, whether in the "i" or "i" variant, and the growing practice in both Europe and other regions, especially where the Latin alphabet is less or not used, of the sign being accompanied by a question mark;

Considering, however, that the actual status of the sign is not always clear to its current and potential users and beneficiaries;

1. **Reaffirms said recommendation** to use the "i" (or "i") sign, as shown in the appendix, in order to:
   (a) indicate the location of public tourist information offices
   (b) indicate all the other places, whether official or private, where tourism information is provided free of charge to the public at large
   (c) indicate the availability of tourist information in printed, audio-visual and electronic media.
2. **Recommends** to alternatively use in these instances the "i" (or "i") sign accompanied by a question mark as shown in appendix 2.

Appendix 1
The tourist information sign

Model sign A

Model sign B

Appendix 2
The tourist information sign

Model sign A.1

Model sign B.1

b. Draft recommendation on the use of uniform colour referents for beach flag warning systems

The Executive Council

Considering that the present range of colours used for beach flag warning systems confuses international visitors engaging in swimming activities;

Recognizing that this situation presents serious problems to their safety, and gives rise to liability concerns on the part of tour and leisure facility operators;

Recommends to use uniform colour referents for beach flag warning systems, whether for sea or fresh water activities, as follows:

Green: Safe
Yellow: Caution
Red: Danger

c. Draft recommendation on the use of uniform colour referents for outdoor recreation activities and facilities

The Executive Council,

Considering that, at the international level, the range of colour referents presently used to determine the status of difficulty in outdoor recreation activities and corresponding facilities (walking and hiking tracks, trekking, jogging, etc.) is not uniform;

Considering further that this situation may be confusing and even dangerous for international travellers engaging in outdoor recreation activities;

Considering also that the operators of outdoor recreation activities and corresponding facilities interested in making said activities and facilities available and in providing service to international visitors need guidance about the standard colours they could use in communicating the difficulty status of the activities and facilities in question;

Recommends to use uniform colour referents as follows:

Green: Easy
Yellow: Moderate
Red: Difficult
Black: Very difficult and dangerous

d. Draft recommendation on the use of uniform colour referents for ski and winter sports related activities and facilities

The Executive Council,

Considering that, at the international level, the range of colour referents presently used to determine the status of difficulty in ski and winter sports related activities and corresponding facilities (downhill skiing, ski tourism trails, snowboarding, etc.) is not uniform;

Considering further that this situation may be confusing and even dangerous for international visitors engaging in ski and winter sports related activities;

Considering also that the operators of ski and other winter sports related activities and corresponding facilities interested in making said activities and facilities available and in providing service to international visitors need guidance about the standard colours they could use in communicating the difficulty status of the activities and facilities in question;

Recommends to use uniform colour referents as follows:

Green: Easy
Yellow: Moderate
Red: Difficult
Black: Very difficult and dangerous

BIBLIOGRAPHY

ARGENTINA
Argentina, Manual de Señalización Turística, cop., Buenos Aires (undated).
Argentina, El país de los seis continentes, Identidad Corporativa Turística, Manual de Aplicación, Secretaría de Turismo, Presidencia de la Nación, Buenos Aires (undated).

AUSTRALIA
Australia, Western Australian Tourism Commission, Guidelines for Tourism Signs, June 1995, ISBN 0 7309 6463 9.

BOLIVIA
Ministerio de Desarrollo Económico, Secretarìa Nacional de Turismo, Metodología para la Señalización Turística, Dirección de la Planificación, La Paz, Bolivia, Agosto 1997.

EUROPEAN COMMISSION
Council Recommendation of 22 December 1986 on standardized information in existing hotels (86/665/EEC), Official Journal of the European Communities, No. L 384/54, 31/12/86.

FRANCE
Charte Graphique pour panneaux de balisage informatif, Signalétique, Ministère du tourisme, France, Paris, 1993.
Ministère du Tourisme et Ministère de l'Equipement, du Logement et des Transports, Signalisation touristique, Guide, Direction des Journaux Officiels, Paris, France, Mars 1992.
Péter Gérard, chargé de mission SEATER (Ministère du Tourisme), La signalisation touristique en France est-elle pour demain?, polycopié , Paris, Mars 1986.
Signalisation et Signalétique touristiques, numéro spécial d'Espaces, Revue technique du tourisme et des loisirs, Paris, n° 136, novembre - décembre 1995.

INTERNATIONAL ORGANIZATIONS
APEC, Standardization of Symbols for Visitor Signage Final Report, Singapore, May 1999
APEC, Standardization of Symbols for Visitor Signage, Executive Summary, Singapore, May 1999.
COUNCIL OF EUROPE/CONSEIL DE L'EUROPE, Conseil de la Coopération culturelle, Itinéraires culturels européens, ICE (89)1, Strasbourg, Janvier 1989.

ICAO-IMO, International signs to provide guidance to persons at airports and marine terminals, ICAO, IMO, London 1995, IMO sales number: IMO-370M/ ICAO sales number: Doc 9636-C/1

IFTO, Inquiry on Beach Safety, International Federation of Tour Operators, London, April 1997.

IMO, The use of graphical signs and symbols at marine terminals and on board ship, Facilitation Committee, FAL 18/7/1, 7 July 1988, International Maritime Organization.

ISO, International Organization for Standardization, Procedures for the development and testing of public information symbols, ISO 9186: 1989 (E), Geneva, 1989.

UNCRT, United Nations Conference on Road Traffic, Final act and related documents, E/CONF.56/16/.Rev. 1 -17/ Rev. 1 /19, New York 1969.

WIPO, Implications of the TRIPS Agreement on Treaties administered by WIPO, World Intellectual Property Organization, Geneva, 1996.

WTO, Report on the normalization of tourism signs and symbols, PV(VI)B.5.1., Madrid, 22 November 1989, Original: English.

WTO, Second International Conference on Senior Tourism, Recife (Brazil), Proceedings - Selected Materials, Madrid, May 1997 (in particular, see Hal Norvell, AARP, Strategies for Targeting the Senior Market).

WTO, Report on the Status of Tourist Signs and Symbols worldwide , Madrid, 1998.

WTO & ETTFA, Travel & Tourism Fairs, Guideline for Exhibitors, WTO, Madrid, 1997.

PERU
Peru, Manual de Señalización Turística, Sector Turismo, Ministerio de Industria, Comercio Exterior, Turismo e Integración (2™ edición), 1991.

PORTUGAL
Portugal, Manual de identidade, Direcão de Informaão Turística, Lisboa, s.d. Gabinete de Estudos e planeamento, Normalizaão da simbolizai turística, Direcão Geral do Turismo, Lisboa, Outubro 1996.

SPAIN
Turespaña, Desarrollo del logotipo español, Secretaría General de Turismo Madrid (undated).

Dirección General de Carreteras, Ministerio de Fomento, Sistema de señalización turística homologada en las carreteras estatales (SISTHO), Madrid, 1999, 12p.

Dirección General de Carreteras, Ministerio de Fomento y Globalesco, Sistema de señalización turística homologada en las carreteras estatales (SISTHO), Resumen Desarrollo Proyecto, propuestas de diseños, ejemplos aplicados, Madrid, 1999, 15 p.

Dirección general de turismo, Ministerio de Económica y Hacienda, Secretaria de Estado de Comercio, Turismo y de la Pequeña y Mediana Empresa, Información general sobre el sistema de señalización turística homologada (SISTHO), Madrid, 1999, 5 p.

UNITED KINGDOM

British Tourist Authority, Symbols for tourist guides, maps and countryside recreation, Fourth Edition, London, 1993.

British Standards Institute, Public Information Symbols, Proposed British Standard, London, 1997, 4 p.

HMSO, British Government, The Traffic Signs Regulations and General Directions 1994, Statutory Instruments 1994 nº1519, London, 1994.